I0759622

IT'S TIME TO BAKE

cookies

BRIAN HART HOFFMAN

IT'S TIME TO BAKE

cookies

Chocolate chip, oatmeal cream, and everything in between

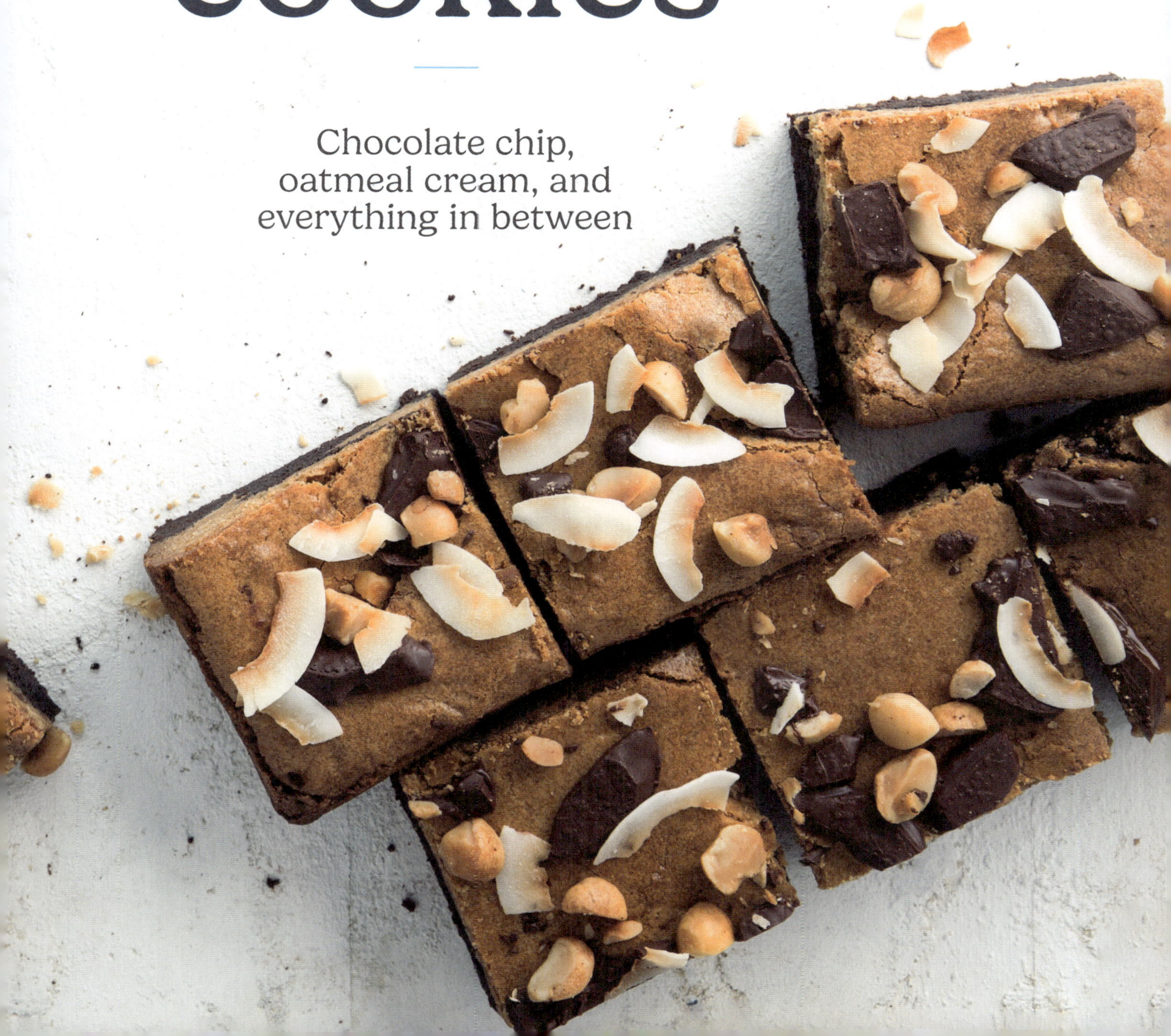

83
press®

83 Press
2323 2nd Avenue North
Birmingham, Alabama 35203
83press.com

ISBN: 979-8-9923852-1-2
Printed in China

contents

A Love Affair with Cookies

There is something deeply comforting about a cookie—warm from the oven, a little crisp at the edges, soft and gooey in the center. In this collection, I pay homage to this beloved treat, a simple yet profound pleasure that has graced our homes for generations. Cookies are not just baked goods; they carry with them stories—of places, of people, of memories. From the familiar, buttery crunch of a chocolate chip cookie to more-unexpected combinations, these recipes are born from my own travels, both near and far. Whether it's the gentle spice of a buttery sablé enjoyed in a Parisian café or a frosting- and sprinkle-covered sugar cookie, each bite tells its own tale.

This collection is an invitation to discover the vast world of cookies, each recipe carefully crafted to satisfy every whim. Whether you're craving something chewy, crisp, or somewhere in between, there's a recipe here for every taste. An entire chapter is devoted to perfecting the chocolate chip cookie, with tips on achieving your ideal texture—whether thick and chewy, thin and crispy, or a perfect balance of both. But this collection is about so much more than just the classic chocolate chip cookie; inside, you'll find cookies with a twist—filled, stuffed, and sandwiched creations—along with fruit-forward and spiced varieties that offer something a little unexpected. There are also larger-than-life cookie cakes and skillet cookies, perfect for sharing with family and friends.

And as with everything I bake, I believe that knowing a few tricks can make all the difference. You'll find advice on making cookies ahead of time, clever decorating ideas, and tips on how to store and package your cookies so they stay perfectly fresh for days. This collection is as much about the joy of baking as it is about creating moments of connection through sharing food. It's a practical guide, but one that is brimming with warmth and love.

Whether you're an experienced baker or taking your first steps into the kitchen, I hope these recipes inspire you to fill your home with the irresistible aroma of freshly baked cookies. And with every batch you bake, I hope you create not only delicious treats but also memories of time spent with those you cherish.

It's time to bake!

Brian

LET'S TALK

cookies

Whether they're chewy, crisp, or somewhere in between, there's no denying that cookies hold a special place in our hearts. But have you ever stopped to wonder: Where did the name "cookie" come from? And why do we call them "cookies" in the US but "biscuits" in other parts of the world?

Let's start with the word "cookie"—it comes from the Dutch word "koekje," meaning "little cake." It all began with Dutch settlers in the American colonies, who would test their cakes by baking small amounts of batter to check the temperature. By the 19th century, cookies became a beloved staple of American culinary culture, defined by their sweet dough, often enriched with sugar, butter, and flavorings.

The word "biscuit" dates back to the 14th century in Europe and comes from the Latin "bis coctus," meaning "twice-cooked," referring to early dry, crunchy breads baked twice to preserve them. In the United Kingdom and much of the world, what Americans call a cookie is a biscuit. On the other hand, in the US, "biscuit" refers to the soft, fluffy quick bread we (particularly Southerners) love for breakfast—two completely different things, all thanks to the way language and culture evolved.

What makes a cookie so special, though, is its sheer versatility. At its core, a cookie is simply a small, sweetened baked good made from dough or batter, but the magic happens with the ingredients—the rich chocolate chips, the crunchy nuts, the warming spices, or the tangy dried fruit. The possibilities are endless. You might crave the buttery thickness of shortbread, the gooey decadence of double chocolate chip, or the comforting spices of a gingersnap. There's a cookie for every taste and every craving.

And whether you're munching on a biscuit or a cookie, one thing's certain: These treats have stood the test of time. They've evolved with us, from small bites to grand celebrations, creating joy, connection, and comfort across generations. After all, cookies aren't just baked goods—they're little moments of happiness, waiting to be shared.

Mastering Cookie Perfection

In the pursuit of cookie excellence, sticking to foundational principles can transform your baking. Here are 10 essential guidelines to elevate your cookie creations.

1 **Test your oven temperature.** Use an oven thermometer to confirm your oven's temperature accuracy, ensuring cookies bake at the correct temperature for optimal results.

2 **Toast nuts before adding.** Lightly toasting nuts before incorporating them into your cookie dough enhances their flavor. Let them cool completely before mixing them into the dough to maintain the desired texture.

3 **Weigh your ingredients accurately.** Using a kitchen scale to weigh your ingredients, especially flour, ensures precise measurements. This practice leads to consistent results and helps achieve the desired texture in your cookies.

4 **Avoid overmixing the dough.** Overmixing can incorporate too much air into the dough or overwork it, leading to cookies that collapse during baking or turn out tough. Mix until ingredients are just combined to achieve the desired texture.

5 **Use a scoop for uniformity.** Using a portion scoop ensures that each cookie is the same size, promoting even baking and a professional appearance.

6 **Chill the dough for enhanced flavor and texture.** Refrigerating your cookie dough for at least 30 minutes before baking allows the flour to hydrate and the fats to solidify. This process minimizes spreading during baking and enhances the overall flavor and texture of the cookies.

7 **Incorporate resting time.** Allowing your dough to rest at room temperature for about 10 minutes before baking can help achieve the perfect spread and texture.

8 **Bake on parchment paper.** Lining your baking sheets with parchment paper prevents cookies from sticking and facilitates easy cleanup.

9 **Rotate baking sheets for even baking.** If baking two pans of cookies at the same time, rotate the pans 180 degrees and swap their positions between the upper and lower racks halfway through the baking time. This ensures even baking and uniformly colored cookies.

10 **Let your oven return to temperature between batches.** Between baking batches, let your oven return to the recipe's specified temperature to ensure consistent baking results.

Essential Ingredients

Excellent cookies require wonderful ingredients. Here are the ingredients I use most often in my cookies.

Unbleached all-purpose flour: Flour is the foundation of nearly all baked goods. Selecting unbleached all-purpose flour from esteemed mills such as Bob's Red Mill or King Arthur ensures a pure, robust base. These flours, free from chemical bleaching agents, impart a natural, hearty flavor and contribute to the desired structure in your bakes.

European-style butter: Butter is not merely a fat; it's a flavor carrier. European-style butters such as Kerrygold, Président, and Plugrà, with their higher butterfat content (around 82%), offer a richness and depth that standard butters lack. This elevated fat percentage results in a creamier texture and a more pronounced, cultured flavor, enhancing the overall profile of your baked goods.

Full-fat dairy products: Full-fat dairy, including creams and whole milk, introduces a luxurious mouthfeel and enhances the flavor complexity of cookies. The higher fat content contributes to tenderness and moisture, ensuring your cookies are decadent without being greasy.

Sugar: Sugar's role in baking extends beyond mere sweetness; it imparts moisture, fosters caramelization, and bestows a golden hue upon cookies. Selecting high-quality sugars, such as C&H and Domino, enhances both the flavor and texture of your cookies.

Salt: Salt is the unsung hero, elevating and balancing flavors. Choosing the right type of salt is crucial, as different salts have varying grain sizes and salinity levels, affecting the final taste and texture. I use Diamond Crystal Kosher Salt for baking and Maldon Sea Salt for a finishing touch.

Pure extracts: Essences like vanilla and almond are the invisible threads connecting flavors. Using pure extracts, as opposed to synthetic versions, imparts authenticity and depth. Neilsen-Massey is an excellent choice.

Leavening agents: Ensuring your leavening agents—baking soda and baking powder—are fresh is essential for achieving the desired texture and rise in your cookies. Store them in airtight containers in a cool, dry place to maintain their potency. Before baking, test their effectiveness: Mix 1 teaspoon (5 grams) baking soda with 1 tablespoon (15 grams) vinegar; if it bubbles vigorously, it's active. For baking powder, combine 1 teaspoon (5 grams) baking powder with ½ cup (120 grams) hot water; a strong fizz confirms it's still potent. Regularly checking the "best by" dates and performing these simple tests will ensure your cookies achieve the perfect rise and texture.

Fresh spices: Spices are the storytellers, adding warmth and complexity. Incorporating freshly ground spices ensures that their oils are intact, delivering a potency and vibrancy that the dusty spices hidden in the depths of your pantry cannot match. If your spices are more than a year old, replace them with fresh.

Quality fruit spreads: Jams and preserves can add a touch of elegance and depth to your cookie creations. Opting for high-quality fruit spreads made from fresh, whole fruits and minimal sweeteners, such as those from Bonne Maman, provide a wonderful flavor and a pleasing texture that complements many baked goods.

WILLIAMS SONOMA
ZWILLING

Essential Equipment

Trusty tools to start you off right

Scale: Precise measuring of ingredients is your first step to baking success. I like a digital scale with a platform wide enough to support a large bowl and still see the readout clearly.

Stand mixer: A stand mixer is indispensable when making cookies, as its robust motor and versatile attachments effortlessly handle even the most demanding doughs. A stand mixer not only enhances efficiency but also elevates the consistency and quality of your dough.

Spring-loaded scoop: Portion and drop dough with ease, precision, and consistent sizing for even baking.

Metal cookie cutters: Thick metal cutters go cleanly through dough without catching or denting. Simpler designs will maintain their shape better during baking than intricate patterns. You can also use a round cutter to gently swirl around cookies hot from the oven to coax them into a perfect circle.

Rolling pin: A long barrel with a uniform thickness allows you to make fewer passes, which means less rolling of dough and more-tender cookies after baking.

Baking sheets: A set of light-colored baking sheets allows you to rotate pans in and out of the oven without any wait time.

Parchment paper: Parchment paper protects the bottom of your cookies from burning and keeps your baking sheets clean. Plus, you can use parchment paper for several rounds of baking; toss it when the edges begin to brown.

Metal and silicone spatulas: A small thin offset spatula lets you delicately handle cutout dough without damaging its shape, and a flat, wide spatula gets fully and securely under baked cookies when transferring them from baking sheets to wire racks. Silicone spatulas let you scrape every last bit of dough off the paddle and out of the mixing bowl.

Wire racks: Wire racks allow air to circulate around cookies so they cool quickly and evenly. Choose racks with a tight grid for proper support so cookies don't sag in the center or on the sides as they cool.

Make and Save

Plan ahead for cookies at the ready

Rolled, dropped, and shaped: Place cookie dough balls or cutout shapes on parchment paper-lined baking sheets, and freeze until they're firm. Once firm, transfer them to a heavy-duty resealable plastic bag, and freeze for up to 3 months. Be sure to label and date the bag. Bake frozen cookie dough as the recipe directs, adding 2 to 3 minutes to the baking time.

Slice-and-bake: Wrap dough logs tightly in plastic wrap and then place in a heavy-duty resealable plastic bag. Label and date the bag, and freeze for up to 3 months. Let the dough thaw in the refrigerator until it's sliceable but still firm; slice and bake as directed.

Bake and Store

Assemble your homemade goodies for gifting

Tins and boxes: Choose a container made of sturdy material to protect your cookies from breaking and that can fully seal to keep food fresh.

Protective papers: Line your containers with food-safe decorative tissue, parchment, or wax paper to help prevent breaking and in between layers of cookies to keep them from sticking to each other.

Like with like: Keep crispy with crispy, spiced with spiced, and so on. Mixing different types or tastes of cookies can cause crispy cookies to become soft or flavors to meld with each other.

Pantry to Pan

Follow this overview of creating perfectly mixed cookie dough for baking, accurately filling and stuffing cookies so they remain intact, and building a sensational sandwich cookie

Making the Dough

Creaming butter, incorporating eggs, and adding flour are all simple but key parts of making cookies. Here's how to execute each step flawlessly.

Creaming together butter and sugar: This step is where softened butter and sugar are beaten not just for the purpose of mixing them together but to incorporate precious air into the dough. Science-wise, the sharp sugar crystals break into the dense fat of the butter, creating little pockets. The mixer simultaneously fills these voids with air, creating microscopic bubbles that expand and lighten the butter-sugar mixture. Every minute you mix, more air is incorporated—but take time to stop and scrape. Certain spots of butter will stubbornly stick to the mixer's paddle and the bottom and sides of the bowl, not getting properly incorporated. If not scraped before creaming is done, these leftover spots become dreaded butter streaks in your cookie dough, creating greasy pockets in some cookies.

Regarding consistency, properly creamed butter and sugar will be fluffy and pale tan in color if using brown sugar or pale yellow if using just granulated sugar. Creamed too little, it'll look and feel like gritty clumps of sand, making cookies that'll spread more and have a denser texture. Butter that has been creamed too much will look soupy and greasy, as the butter will begin to separate from the mixture. This will lead to gummy cookies. You can't salvage over-creamed butter, so pay attention to the changing consistency of your creamed mixture carefully.

Adding eggs: Add eggs, one at a time, beating well after each addition and stopping to scrape the paddle and the sides and bottom of the bowl. The cleanest, easiest way to add eggs to your batter is to place them in a measuring cup and then pour them in one at time. The spout of the measuring cup helps direct the egg flow gradually and directly into the batter so they don't hit and cling to the sides of the bowl or pour out all at once.

Why beat them in one at a time? Eggs are emulsifiers, which means they help bind ingredients together to create a homogenous mixture. However, if you add them all at once, they emulsify with each other first, creating a large, scrambled mixture that resists smooth incorporation. Make it easier on your dough and add them gradually.

Beating in extracts: The last thing to add to the wet ingredients is your extracts. Extracts don't distribute as thoroughly in the thicker, flour-incorporated dough. You'd have to mix longer, which creates a tougher cookie.

Whisking together dry ingredients: There's no need to sift your dry ingredients together for cookies. A bowl, a whisk, and a quick stir are all that's needed to ensure the dry ingredients are well combined.

Gradually adding dry ingredients to wet ingredients: We've all been there. Your mixer speed was still on medium, you added the flour, and the rapid movement caused the flour to fly up into your face and out of the bowl. So, be sure to reduce the mixer speed to low.

The process of "just until combined" is fast but gentle. It might not even take a minute for your dry ingredients to be properly incorporated into the wet ingredients. Once there are no more streaks of flour, stop mixing your dough, as every second mixing activates more gluten in the flour, making the dough tough.

Stuffing Cookies

Stuffing involves incorporating a filling directly into the cookie dough before baking, resulting in a cookie with a surprise inside.

Here's how you can achieve this:

1 Place a small amount of filling in the center of a portion of dough; you don't want so much filling that your dough cannot cover it.

2 Carefully wrap the dough around the filling, pinching the edges to seal to prevent leakage during baking.

3 Roll your stuffed dough pieces into balls or disks as the recipe indicates to ensure a smooth exterior that does not leak.

Sandwiching Cookies

Sandwiching entails joining two cookies together with a filling. This method allows for a variety of textures and flavors.

Here's how to create sandwich cookies:

1. Turn your cooled baked cookies flat side up.

2. Spoon about 1 tablespoon of filling onto the flat side of one cookie. If you're piping the filling, start in the center of the cookie and move in a spiral outward.

3. Place another cookie, flat side down, onto the filling. Gently press the cookies together or twist them in opposite directions to distribute the filling evenly to the edges of the cookies.

4. Let the sandwiched cookies stand for a few minutes before serving to ensure the filling adheres well.

Chocolate Chip Cookies

EVERY WHICH WAY

The classic chocolate chip cookie is reimagined with delightful variations, from an indulgent browned butter version to a graham cracker-infused creation, each offering a fresh perspective on this timeless treat. And, of course, there's also a guide to create *your* own perfect chocolate chip cookie.

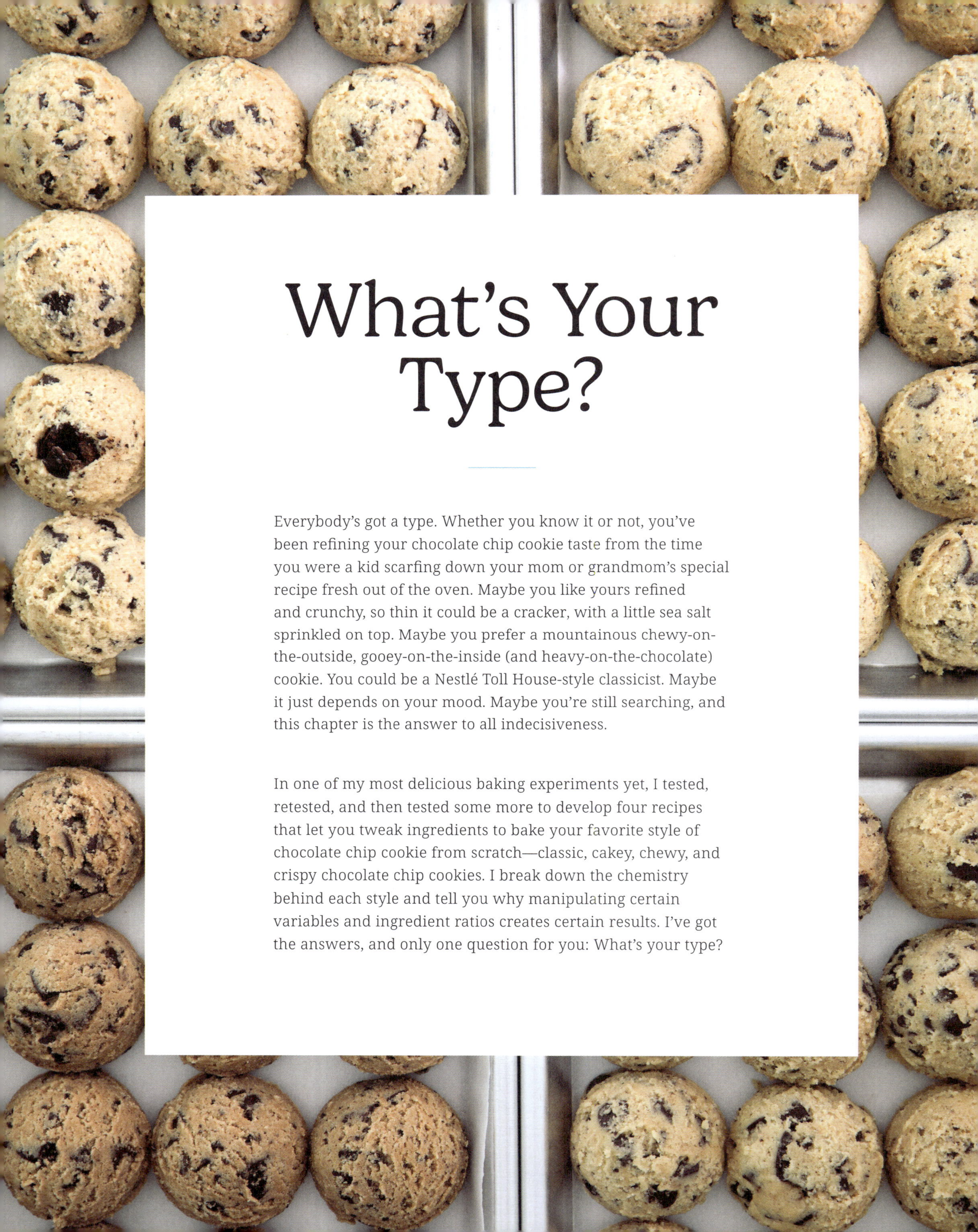

What's Your Type?

Everybody's got a type. Whether you know it or not, you've been refining your chocolate chip cookie taste from the time you were a kid scarfing down your mom or grandmom's special recipe fresh out of the oven. Maybe you like yours refined and crunchy, so thin it could be a cracker, with a little sea salt sprinkled on top. Maybe you prefer a mountainous chewy-on-the-outside, gooey-on-the-inside (and heavy-on-the-chocolate) cookie. You could be a Nestlé Toll House-style classicist. Maybe it just depends on your mood. Maybe you're still searching, and this chapter is the answer to all indecisiveness.

In one of my most delicious baking experiments yet, I tested, retested, and then tested some more to develop four recipes that let you tweak ingredients to bake your favorite style of chocolate chip cookie from scratch—classic, cakey, chewy, and crispy chocolate chip cookies. I break down the chemistry behind each style and tell you why manipulating certain variables and ingredient ratios creates certain results. I've got the answers, and only one question for you: What's your type?

Choose Your Chocolate

The size, shape, and type of chocolate you use will affect the taste and look of your cookie. I use high-quality semisweet chocolate, which has a cacao content of around 60%, and indicates that no more than 50% of the mass of chocolate is sugar.

HAND-CHOPPED

For a more chocolaty cookie, chop a chocolate bar. With roughly chopped flakes and chunks, each bite of your cookie will taste different and there is a wider distribution of chocolate throughout. Hand-chopped chocolate works best in thinner cookies.

CHIPS

For a batch of uniform cookies with chocolate in distinct pockets, use chips. Chips soften and melt a bit but largely retain their shape during baking. They won't spread out into the dough like hand-chopped chocolate, so go with chips if you like more cookie in your bite.

FÈVES

Fèves are oval-shaped disks of chocolate that create pools of melty goodness when baked. They're used most often in professional bakeries and generally are a higher-quality chocolate than chips, but fèves are easy to find online.

Don't Forget the Salt

Salt balances the flavor of the caramelized sugars and gives a simple chocolate chip cookie delicious complexity.

I bake with kosher salt, but if you use table salt or another fine-grain salt, cut the salt measurement of the recipe in half. If you like, sprinkle a little flaked sea salt on your cookies right out of the oven for even more salty-sweet flavor contrast.

Know the Dough

How you handle your cookie dough is just as important as what you put in it.

LESS KNEADING = BETTER TEXTURE

The less you work the dough, the softer your cookies will be. It's best to barely work the flour in, mixing it just until a dough comes together. Overworking creates stronger gluten networks, which leads to a tough texture.

LONGER REST = BETTER FLAVOR

A longer rest time before baking gives your cookies more complex, concentrated flavor, reminiscent of toffee or butterscotch. The flour proteins and starches have time to break down. Ingredients can marinate and soak up extra moisture, so the flavors become more pronounced.

LONGER REST = MORE COMPACT

Chilling the dough before baking solidifies the fat in the cookies. Solid fat takes longer to melt than room temperature fat, so cookies made with chilled dough will spread less.

Oven Temperature

The most common baking temperature is 350°F (180°C), but it's not a requirement.

HIGHER THAN 350°F (180°C)

You'll have darker, more-compact cookies. Caramelization occurs above 356°F (180°C) and gives cookies their tanned exterior, crunchier texture, and more caramel flavor.

LOWER THAN 350°F (180°C)

When baking low and slow, you'll have wider cookies and an even consistency from the edges to the center of the cookie. Ingredients don't get hot enough to bind to one another and form a firm structure during the beginning of baking, so they continue to spread.

At-a-Glance Guide

Chart your course for your ideal cookie

	Flour	Butter	Sugar	Leavener	Eggs (LARGE)
Classic	All-Purpose	Softened	Equal Volumes of Brown and Granulated = Soft Center, Crisp Edges	Baking Powder + Baking Soda = Soft Center, Crisp Edges	2
Cakey	All-Purpose + Cake Flour = More Height	Softened + Less Butter = Less Spread, More Height	More Brown + Even Less Granulated = Soft, Thick Texture	Baking Soda + Baking Powder = More Rise, Airy Texture	2 + Milk = Softer Texture
Chewy	All-Purpose + Bread Flour (More Protein) + Cornstarch = More Chew	Melted = Less Air in Dough = Moist and Compact	Much More Brown Than Granulated = Soft, Moist Texture	Less Baking Soda = Denser Cookie	1 Whole + 1 Yolk = More Protein
Crispy	All-Purpose	Softened + Bake at Higher Temp to Melt Fast = More Spread	Granulated Only = Minimal Moisture for More Crunch	Baking Soda	2

Classic These cookies are the great equalizer, incorporating a bit of character from the other types, and most similar to what you'd get if you baked the recipe on the back of a bag of Nestlé Toll House chocolate chips. Equal volumes of brown sugar and granulated sugar create crispy edges and a chewy center. A standard amount of all-purpose flour and leavener create just a touch of airy texture. A little softness, a little crunch, and a little chew.

Cakey The airiest and lightest of the bunch, the cakey cookies have more flour than the rest, which gives them more height. Adding lower-protein cake flour with all-purpose flour keeps the cookies soft since cake flour produces less gluten. To compensate for the extra flour, milk is added, which helps tenderize the dough. Both baking powder and baking soda are used for height; as the cakey cookies bake, the powder and soda break down into carbon dioxide gas, which makes the dough rise. These gases also leave little holes in the cookies, making them lighter. The higher the proportion of butter to other ingredients, the more the cookies will spread as they bake, so I reduced the butter and granulated sugar (which promotes crispness) to help keep these cookies thick and supple.

Chewy Most of the chewy cookies' chew comes from the addition of cornstarch and substituting bread flour for some of the all-purpose flour. Bread flour has more protein than all-purpose flour, which helps with gluten development. The more gluten you have, the denser your cookie will be. Reducing the amount of egg whites helps thicken the dough by removing some moisture and reduces the amount of spread. When cooked, egg yolk forms a protein shell that keeps the cookies' interior tender and gives them a chewy texture throughout. Using melted butter reduces the amount of air creamed into the batter, which keeps the cookies compact and moist.

Crispy When you break one of these crispy cookies, you'll have no bend—just a satisfying snap. Using only granulated sugar and baking at a higher temperature are the main factors that give these cookies their lightness and crunch. Using baking soda rather than baking powder allows the cookies to spread rather than rise during baking.

Almond Flour

Semolina Flour

Whole Wheat Flour

Beyond the 4Cs: The Power of Flour

If you've never met a chocolate chip cookie you didn't love, or you love to experiment and fine-tune *your* one perfect version, by simply swapping the types and amounts of flour in a chocolate chip cookie—while keeping all the other ingredients and their amounts the same—you can achieve distinct benefits in texture and taste. You can find these unique variations in this chapter, too.

Classic Chocolate Chip Cookies

Makes about 24 cookies

These cookies are buttery, caramelly, chocolaty, not overly sweet, a little crisp, and a little soft—true crowd-pleasers.

- **1 cup (227 grams) unsalted butter, softened**
- **¾ cup (150 grams) granulated sugar**
- **¾ cup (165 grams) firmly packed light brown sugar**
- **2 large eggs (100 grams), room temperature**
- **2 teaspoons (8 grams) vanilla extract**
- **2¾ cups (344 grams) all-purpose flour**
- **1 teaspoon (5 grams) baking powder**
- **1 teaspoon (3 grams) kosher salt**
- **½ teaspoon (2.5 grams) baking soda**
- **2 cups (340 grams) semisweet chocolate chips**

1. Line a baking sheet with parchment paper.
2. In the bowl of a stand mixer fitted with the paddle attachment, beat butter and sugars at medium speed until fluffy, 2 to 3 minutes, stopping to scrape paddle and bottom and sides of bowl. Add eggs, one at a time, beating well after each addition. Beat in vanilla.
3. In a medium bowl, whisk together flour, baking powder, salt, and baking soda. With mixer on low speed, gradually add flour mixture to butter mixture, beating just until combined and stopping to scrape paddle and bottom and sides of bowl. Stir in chocolate chips just until combined.
4. Using a 3-tablespoon (about 55 grams) spring-loaded scoop, scoop dough, and place on prepared pan. Cover and refrigerate while oven preheats.
5. Preheat oven to 375°F (190°C). Line baking sheets with parchment paper.
6. Place dough balls 2 inches apart on prepared pans.
7. Bake, one pan at a time, until golden brown, 8 to 10 minutes, rotating pan halfway through baking. Let cool on pan for 5 minutes. Remove from pan, and let cool completely on a wire rack. Store in an airtight container for up to 3 days.

Cakey Chocolate Chip Cookies

Makes about 20 cookies

The dough for these cakey cookies is mixed like a cake batter so their texture is tender with lift. Refrigerating the dough gives the ingredients time to meld together and solidifies the butter, which helps control spreading during baking. And the longer these cookies rest after baking, the softer they become due to absorbing moisture in the air. Let them rest for at least 30 minutes before serving.

- **¾ cup plus 2 tablespoons (198 grams) unsalted butter, softened**
- **1 cup (220 grams) firmly packed light brown sugar**
- **⅓ cup (67 grams) granulated sugar**
- **2 large eggs (100 grams)**
- **2 teaspoons (8 grams) vanilla extract**
- **2 cups (250 grams) all-purpose flour**
- **1 cup (125 grams) cake flour**
- **1 teaspoon (5 grams) baking soda**
- **¾ teaspoon (2.25 grams) kosher salt**
- **½ teaspoon (2.5 grams) baking powder**
- **¼ cup (60 grams) whole milk**
- **2 cups (340 grams) semisweet chocolate chips**

1. Line a rimmed baking sheet with parchment paper.
2. In the bowl of a stand mixer fitted with the paddle attachment, beat butter and sugars at medium speed until fluffy, 3 to 4 minutes, stopping to scrape paddle and bottom and sides of bowl. Reduce mixer speed to medium-low. Add eggs, one at a time, beating well after each addition. Beat in vanilla.
3. In a medium bowl, whisk together flours, baking soda, salt, and baking powder. With mixer on low speed, gradually add flour mixture to butter mixture alternately with milk, beginning and ending with flour mixture, beating just until combined after each addition and stopping to scrape paddle and bottom and sides of bowl. (Do not overmix; dough will be soft.) Gently stir in chocolate chips.
4. Using a 3-tablespoon scoop, scoop dough, and place on prepared pan. Cover and refrigerate for at least 3 hours or up to overnight.
5. Preheat oven to 350°F (180°C). Line baking sheets with parchment paper.
6. Place dough balls 2 inches apart on prepared pans.
7. Bake, one pan at a time, until edges are golden brown, 15 to 18 minutes, rotating pan halfway through baking. Let cool on pan for 5 minutes. Remove from pan, and let cool completely on a wire rack. Store in an airtight container for up to 3 days.

Chewy Chocolate Chip Cookies

Makes about 26 cookies

These stay soft and flexible even as they cool straight out of the oven—the ultimate satisfaction for chewy cookie devotees.

- **1 cup (220 grams) firmly packed light brown sugar**
- **¾ cup (170 grams) unsalted butter, melted**
- **⅔ cup (133 grams) granulated sugar**
- **1 large egg (50 grams)**
- **1 large egg yolk (19 grams)**
- **2 teaspoons (8 grams) vanilla extract**
- **2 cups (250 grams) all-purpose flour**
- **⅓ cup (42 grams) bread flour**
- **2 teaspoons (6 grams) cornstarch**
- **¾ teaspoon (3.75 grams) baking soda**
- **¾ teaspoon (2.25 grams) kosher salt**
- **1½ cups (255 grams) semisweet chocolate chips**

1. Preheat oven to 350°F (180°C). Line baking sheets with parchment paper.
2. In the bowl of a stand mixer fitted with the paddle attachment, beat brown sugar, melted butter, and granulated sugar at medium speed until combined. Reduce mixer speed to medium-low. Add egg and egg yolk, one at a time, beating well after each addition. Beat in vanilla.
3. In a medium bowl, whisk together flours, cornstarch, baking soda, and salt. With mixer on low speed, gradually add flour mixture to sugar mixture, beating just until combined and stopping to scrape paddle and bottom and sides of bowl. (Do not overmix.) Gently stir in chocolate chips.
4. Using a 1½-tablespoon spring-loaded scoop, scoop two-thirds of dough, and place 2 inches apart on prepared pans. Spoon 1½ teaspoons dough onto each dough portion on pans. Lightly press dough portions together.
5. Bake, one pan at a time, until edges are just beginning to brown but centers still look a little wet, 10 to 12 minutes, rotating pan halfway through baking. Let cool on pan for 5 minutes. Remove from pan, and let cool completely on a wire rack. Store in an airtight container for up to 3 days.

Crispy Chocolate Chip Cookies

Makes about 20 cookies

Giving the baking sheet a firm whack on a countertop halfway through baking makes the final result even thinner for more crunch.

- **1 cup (227 grams) unsalted butter, softened**
- **1½ cups (300 grams) granulated sugar**
- **2 large eggs (100 grams)**
- **2 teaspoons (8 grams) vanilla extract**
- **2¼ cups plus 3 tablespoons (305 grams) all-purpose flour**
- **1 teaspoon (5 grams) baking soda**
- **¾ teaspoon (2.25 grams) kosher salt**
- **1⅓ cups (227 grams) semisweet chocolate chips**

1. Preheat oven to 375°F (190°C). Line baking sheets with parchment paper.
2. In the bowl of a stand mixer fitted with the paddle attachment, beat butter and sugar at medium speed until fluffy, 3 to 4 minutes, stopping to scrape paddle and bottom and sides of bowl. Reduce mixer speed to medium-low. Add eggs, one at a time, beating well after each addition. Beat in vanilla.
3. In a medium bowl, whisk together flour, baking soda, and salt. With mixer on low speed, gradually add flour mixture to butter mixture, beating just until combined and stopping to scrape paddle and bottom and sides of bowl. (Do not overmix.) Gently stir in chocolate chips.
4. Using a 3-tablespoon scoop, scoop dough, and place 2 inches apart on prepared pans. Gently press each dough portion to flatten to half its original height.
5. Bake, one pan at a time, until edges are golden brown, 15 to 18 minutes, rotating pan and banging pan on countertop halfway through baking to help cookies spread. Let cool on pan for 5 minutes. Remove from pan, and let cool completely on a wire rack. Store in an airtight container for up to 3 days.

Almond Flour Chocolate Chip Cookies

Makes about 26 cookies

Nutty, rich almond flour brings a boost of flavor and texture to these cookies. This recipe calls for an addition of baking powder, which helps the heavier almond flour dough rise. Plus, there's no need to flatten your dough balls into disks; they spread well all on their own.

- **1 cup (227 grams) unsalted butter, softened**
- **1 cup (220 grams) firmly packed light brown sugar**
- **½ cup (100 grams) granulated sugar**
- **2 large eggs (100 grams), room temperature**
- **2 teaspoons (8 grams) vanilla extract**
- **2 cups (192 grams) superfine almond flour**
- **1¾ cups (219 grams) all-purpose flour**
- **1 teaspoon (5 grams) baking soda**
- **1 teaspoon (3 grams) kosher salt**
- **½ teaspoon (2.5 grams) baking powder**
- **2 cups (340 grams) semisweet chocolate chips**

1. Line a rimmed baking sheet with parchment paper.
2. In the bowl of a stand mixer fitted with the paddle attachment, beat butter and sugars at medium speed until fluffy, 2 to 3 minutes, stopping to scrape paddle and bottom and sides of bowl. Add eggs, one at a time, beating well after each addition and stopping to scrape paddle and bottom and sides of bowl. Beat in vanilla.
3. In a medium bowl, whisk together flours, baking soda, salt, and baking powder. With mixer on low speed, gradually add flour mixture to butter mixture, beating just until combined and stopping to scrape paddle and bottom and sides of bowl. Beat in chocolate chips just until combined.
4. Using a 3-tablespoon (about 50 grams) spring-loaded scoop, scoop dough, and place on prepared pan. Cover and refrigerate for at least 2 hours or overnight.
5. Preheat oven to 350°F (180°C). Line baking sheets with parchment paper.
6. Place dough balls 2 inches apart on prepared pans.
7. Bake, one pan at a time, until bottom edges are golden brown, 8 to 12 minutes, rotating pan halfway through baking. Let cool on pan for 5 minutes. Remove from pan, and let cool completely on a wire rack. Store in an airtight container for up to 3 days.

Semolina Chocolate Chip Cookies

Makes about 26 cookies

A blend of all-purpose and semolina flours transforms this recipe into a golden-hued standout. Semolina pumps up the buttery color and flavor of these cookies, in addition to giving them a toothsome crumb. The high baking temperature helps the cookies spread more, so you can keep your cookie dough balls in mounds.

---

1 cup (227 grams) unsalted butter, softened
1 cup (220 grams) firmly packed light brown sugar
½ cup (100 grams) granulated sugar
2 large eggs (100 grams), room temperature
2 teaspoons (8 grams) vanilla extract
1½ cups (188 grams) all-purpose flour
1 cup (180 grams) semolina flour
1 teaspoon (5 grams) baking soda
1 teaspoon (3 grams) kosher salt
2 cups (340 grams) semisweet chocolate chips

1. Line a rimmed baking sheet with parchment paper.
2. In the bowl of a stand mixer fitted with the paddle attachment, beat butter and sugars at medium speed until fluffy, 2 to 3 minutes, stopping to scrape paddle and bottom and sides of bowl. Add eggs, one at a time, beating well after each addition and stopping to scrape paddle and bottom and sides of bowl. Beat in vanilla.
3. In a medium bowl, whisk together flours, baking soda, and kosher salt. With mixer on low speed, gradually add flour mixture to butter mixture, beating just until combined and stopping to scrape paddle and bottom and sides of bowl. Beat in chocolate chips just until combined.
4. Using a 3-tablespoon (about 50 grams) spring-loaded scoop, scoop dough, and place on prepared pan. Cover and refrigerate for at least 2 hours or overnight.
5. Preheat oven to 400°F (200°C). Line baking sheets with parchment paper.
6. Place dough balls 2 inches apart on prepared pans.
7. Bake, one pan at a time, until golden brown, 8 to 12 minutes, rotating pan halfway through baking. Let cool on pan for 5 minutes. Remove from pan, and let cool completely on a wire rack. Store in an airtight container for up to 3 days.

Whole Wheat Chocolate Chip Cookies

Makes about 26 cookies

Packing earthy whole wheat flavor and a robust protein content for plenty of chew, these cookies bake at a higher temperature than many others. Be sure you check the bottoms of the cookies, not the tops, for signs of doneness.

1 cup (227 grams) unsalted butter, softened
1 cup (220 grams) firmly packed light brown sugar
½ cup (100 grams) granulated sugar
2 large eggs (100 grams), room temperature
2 teaspoons (8 grams) vanilla extract
3 cups (375 grams) whole wheat flour
1 teaspoon (5 grams) baking soda
1 teaspoon (3 grams) kosher salt
2 cups (340 grams) mini semisweet chocolate chips

1. Line a rimmed baking sheet with parchment paper.
2. In the bowl of a stand mixer fitted with the paddle attachment, beat butter and sugars at medium speed until fluffy, 2 to 3 minutes, stopping to scrape paddle and bottom and sides of bowl. Add eggs, one at a time, beating well after each addition and stopping to scrape paddle and bottom and sides of bowl. Beat in vanilla.
3. In a medium bowl, whisk together flour, baking soda, and kosher salt. With mixer on low speed, gradually add flour mixture to butter mixture, beating just until combined and stopping to scrape paddle and bottom and sides of bowl. Beat in chocolate chips just until combined.
4. Using a 3-tablespoon (about 50 grams) spring-loaded scoop, scoop dough, and place on prepared pan. Cover and refrigerate for at least 2 hours or overnight.
5. Preheat oven to 375°F (190°C). Line baking sheets with parchment paper.
6. Press dough balls into 2¼-inch disks, making sure edges are even. Place 2 inches apart on prepared pans.
7. Bake, one pan at a time, until bottom edges are golden brown, 8 to 12 minutes, rotating pan halfway through baking. Let cool on pan for 5 minutes. Remove from pan, and let cool completely on a wire rack. Store in an airtight container for up to 3 days.

My Ultimate Chocolate Chip Cookies

Makes about 34 cookies

I sometimes describe these as grown-up chocolate chip cookies. The fèves melt into oozy pockets of rich cocoa goodness, and the sprinkle of sea salt adds a subtle crunch and balance of flavor to the sweeteness. No matter how often I bake these, they're always decadently delicious.

---

1 cup (227 grams) unsalted butter, softened
¾ cup (150 grams) granulated sugar
¾ cup (165 grams) firmly packed light brown sugar
2 large eggs (100 grams)
2 teaspoons (8 grams) vanilla extract
2¾ cups (344 grams) all-purpose flour
1 teaspoon (5 grams) baking powder
1 teaspoon (3 grams) kosher salt
¾ teaspoon (3.75 grams) baking soda
2 cups (340 grams) dark chocolate fèves
Garnish: flaked sea salt

1. Line a rimmed baking sheet with parchment paper.
2. In the bowl of a stand mixer fitted with the paddle attachment, beat butter and sugars at medium speed until fluffy, 2 to 3 minutes, stopping to scrape paddle and bottom and sides of bowl. Add eggs, one at a time, beating well after each addition. Beat in vanilla.
3. In a medium bowl, whisk together flour, baking powder, kosher salt, and baking soda. With mixer on low speed, gradually add flour mixture to butter mixture, beating just until combined and stopping to scrape paddle and bottom and sides of bowl. Stir in chocolate.
4. Using a 1½-tablespoon (about 30 grams) spring-loaded scoop, scoop dough, and place on prepared pan. Cover and refrigerate for at least 2 hours or overnight.
5. Preheat oven to 375°F (190°C). Line baking sheets with parchment paper.
6. Place dough balls 2 inches apart on prepared pans.
7. Bake until golden brown, about 8 minutes, rotating pans halfway through baking. Garnish with sea salt, if desired. Let cool on pans for 5 minutes. Remove from pans, and let cool completely on wire racks. Store in an airtight container for up to 3 days.

Chocolate Chip Graham Cookies

Makes about 25 cookies

Love s'mores? Meet your new favorite cookie, which incorporates graham cracker crumbs into the dough to give you two of the three essential s'mores elements in one. Simply add marshmallows and you'll be the hit of the party.

- **1 cup (227 grams) unsalted butter, softened**
- **¾ cup (165 grams) firmly packed dark brown sugar**
- **½ cup (100 grams) granulated sugar**
- **1 tablespoon (21 grams) honey**
- **2 large eggs (100 grams)**
- **1 teaspoon (4 grams) vanilla extract**
- **2⅓ cups (292 grams) all-purpose flour**
- **1 cup (120 grams) graham cracker crumbs**
- **1 teaspoon (5 grams) baking powder**
- **1 teaspoon (3 grams) kosher salt**
- **¾ teaspoon (3.75 grams) baking soda**
- **2 cups (340 grams) semisweet chocolate chips**

1. Preheat oven to 350°F (180°C). Line baking sheets with parchment paper.

2. In the bowl of a stand mixer fitted with the paddle attachment, beat butter and sugars at medium speed until fluffy, 2 to 3 minutes, stopping to scrape paddle and bottom and sides of bowl. Beat in honey. Add eggs, one at a time, beating well after each addition. Beat in vanilla.

3. In a medium bowl, whisk together flour, graham cracker crumbs, baking powder, salt, and baking soda. With mixer on low speed, gradually add flour mixture to butter mixture, beating just until combined and stopping to scrape paddle and bottom and sides of bowl. Stir in chocolate chips.

4. Using a 3-tablespoon (about 54 grams) spring-loaded scoop, scoop dough, and place 2 inches apart on prepared pans.

5. Bake, one pan at a time, until lightly browned, 12 to 14 minutes, rotating pan halfway through baking. Let cool on pan for 5 minutes. Remove from pan, and let cool completely on wire racks. Store in an airtight container for up to 3 days.

Browned Butter Chocolate Chip Cookies

Makes about 24 cookies

The addition of browned butter enhances the caramelly notes of brown sugar and adds a slightly nutty flavor to every bite.

1 cup (227 grams) unsalted butter
¾ cup (150 grams) granulated sugar
½ cup (110 grams) firmly packed light brown sugar
2 large eggs (100 grams)
1 large egg yolk (19 grams)
1 teaspoon (4 grams) vanilla extract
2¾ cups (344 grams) all-purpose flour
1 teaspoon (3 grams) kosher salt
¾ teaspoon (3.75 grams) baking soda
2 cups (340 grams) semisweet chocolate chips
Garnish: flaked sea salt

1. In a medium light-colored skillet, melt butter over medium heat. Cook, stirring occasionally, until butter turns a medium-brown color and has a nutty aroma, about 10 minutes. Remove from heat, and pour into a heatproof bowl. Refrigerate, stirring every 5 minutes, until butter had cooled and solidified but is still a little soft.
2. Line a rimmed baking sheet with parchment paper.
3. In the bowl of a stand mixer fitted with the paddle attachment, beat browned butter and sugars at medium speed until fluffy, 2 to 3 minutes, stopping to scrape paddle and bottom and sides of bowl. Add eggs and egg yolk, one at a time, beating well after each addition. Beat in vanilla.
4. In a medium bowl, whisk together flour, kosher salt, and baking soda. With mixer on low speed, gradually add flour mixture to butter mixture, beating just until combined and stopping to scrape paddle and bottom and sides of bowl. Beat in chocolate chips.
5. Using a 3-tablespoon (about 54 grams) spring-loaded scoop, scoop dough, and place on prepared pan. Cover and refrigerate for at least 2 hours or overnight.
6. Preheat oven to 350°F (180°C). Line baking sheets with parchment paper.
7. Roll chilled dough into smooth balls, and place 2 inches apart on prepared pans.
8. Bake, one pan at a time, until golden brown, 13 to 18 minutes, rotating pan halfway through baking. Garnish with sea salt, if desired. Let cool on pan for 5 minutes. Remove from pan, and let cool completely on a wire rack. Store in an airtight container for up to 3 days.

Browning butter

LESS WATER = MORE FLAVOR

Browning butter does two things: It cooks off water in the butter and caramelizes the milk solids, which is what creates its golden hue and nutty flavor. Water comprises approximately 18% of a stick of butter, which means that browned butter will reduce in volume and weight by approximately 18%, give or take. For example, 100 grams of butter will reduce to about 80 grams of browned butter. Your butter can go from perfectly browned to burnt in a flash, so it's important to pay attention and keep an eye on your pan.

Edible Cookie Dough

Makes 2½ cups

Let's be honest: A nibble or two of dough is half the fun of baking cookies! This egg-free, food-safe base boasts all the hallmarks of chocolate chip cookie dough—molasses-rich dark brown sugar, intense vanilla flavor, and velvety chocolate chunks—without the need for warning labels. I toasted the flour in the oven, as eating raw flour is unsafe, and happily indulged in the touch of nuttiness it brought to this irresistible snack.

- **1½ cups (188 grams) all-purpose flour**
- **⅔ cup (150 grams) unsalted butter, room temperature**
- **1 cup (220 grams) firmly packed dark brown sugar**
- **1 teaspoon (3 grams) kosher salt**
- **2 tablespoons (30 grams) whole milk**
- **1 tablespoon (13 grams) vanilla extract**
- **½ cup (85 grams) chopped dark chocolate**

1. Preheat oven to 350°F (180°C).

2. Spread flour onto a rimmed baking sheet.

3. Bake until very lightly browned, 5 to 7 minutes, gently shaking pan and stirring flour every 2 minutes. Let cool completely on pan.

4. In the bowl of a stand mixer fitted with the paddle attachment, beat butter, brown sugar, and salt at medium speed until fluffy, 3 to 4 minutes, stopping to scrape paddle and bottom and sides of bowl. With mixer on medium-low speed, gradually add toasted flour alternately with milk and vanilla, beginning and ending with toasted flour, beating just until combined after each addition and stopping to scrape paddle and bottom and sides of bowl. Stir in chocolate. Refrigerate in an airtight container for up to 5 days.

Filled, Stuffed, and Sandwiched

These confections conceal delightful surprises, such as zesty citrus curd in Linzers and fruit-studded thumbprints, each exemplifying the joy of hidden indulgences

Linzer Cookies with Meyer Lemon Curd

Makes 36 sandwich cookies

Meyer lemons are slightly sweeter and less acidic than standard lemons and render a curd that's nothing short of magical. I love it sandwiched between cookies—and eaten directly off the spoon.

- 2⅔ cups (333 grams) all-purpose flour
- 1 cup (142 grams) blanched almonds
- ½ cup (100 grams) granulated sugar
- 1 tablespoon (6 grams) Meyer lemon zest
- ½ teaspoon (1.5 grams) kosher salt
- ½ teaspoon (1 gram) ground cinnamon
- ½ teaspoon (1 gram) freshly grated nutmeg
- 1 cup (227 grams) cold unsalted butter
- ½ teaspoon (2 grams) vanilla extract
- Confectioners' sugar, for dusting
- Meyer Lemon Curd (recipe follows)

1. In the work bowl of a food processor, pulse flour, almonds, granulated sugar, lemon zest, salt, cinnamon, and nutmeg until almonds are finely ground. Add cold butter and vanilla, and pulse until mixture is crumbly.

2. Turn out dough, and knead until it comes together. Shape into a disk, and wrap in plastic wrap. Refrigerate for at least 2 hours.

3. Preheat oven to 325°F (170°C). Line baking sheets with parchment paper.

4. Roll dough to ⅛-inch thickness between 2 sheets of parchment paper. Using a 2½-inch round fluted cutter, cut dough, rerolling scraps as necessary. Using a ¾-inch fluted round cutter, cut centers from half of cookies. Place on prepared pans.

5. Bake until golden brown, 13 to 15 minutes. Let cool completely on pans.

6. Dust cooled cookies with cutouts with confectioners' sugar. Spread 2 teaspoons Meyer Lemon Curd onto flat side of all solid cookies. Place cookies with cutouts, flat side down, on top of filling. Serve immediately.

Meyer Lemon Curd

Makes 1½ cups

- ½ cup (100 grams) granulated sugar, divided
- 5 large egg yolks (93 grams)
- 3 tablespoons (18 grams) Meyer lemon zest
- ½ cup (120 grams) fresh Meyer lemon juice (about 3 lemons)
- 5 tablespoons (70 grams) unsalted butter, room temperature

1. In a medium bowl, whisk together ¼ cup (50 grams) sugar, egg yolks, and lemon zest.

2. In a medium saucepan, bring lemon juice and remaining ¼ cup (50 grams) sugar to a boil over medium heat. Add about ¼ cup hot juice mixture to egg yolk mixture, whisking constantly. Add egg yolk mixture to remaining hot juice mixture in pan, whisking until combined. Strain through a fine-mesh sieve, discarding solids.

3. Return mixture to pan, and cook over medium heat, stirring constantly, until thickened, 3 to 4 minutes. Whisk in butter, 1 tablespoon (14 grams) at a time, until combined. Transfer to a heatproof bowl, and refrigerate until completely cool. Cover and refrigerate for up to 1 week.

Cranberry Thumbprint Cookies

Makes about 30 cookies

These charming treats feature a buttery, melt-in-your-mouth cookie topped with a sweet and tangy cranberry filling. Customize them to your liking with any seasonal homemade jam or store-bought flavor you like.

- ¾ cup (170 grams) unsalted butter, softened
- 1¾ cups (210 grams) confectioners' sugar, divided
- 1 teaspoon (3 grams) kosher salt
- 2 large egg yolks (37 grams), room temperature
- ½ teaspoon (2 grams) almond extract
- 2 cups (250 grams) all-purpose flour
- ¼ teaspoon (1.25 grams) baking powder
- 1 tablespoon (15 grams) water
- Quick Cranberry Jam (recipe follows)
- Garnish: orange zest

1. Line baking sheets with parchment paper.
2. In the bowl of a stand mixer fitted with the paddle attachment, beat butter, 1¼ cups (150 grams) confectioners' sugar, and salt at medium speed until fluffy, 2 to 3 minutes, stopping to scrape bottom and sides of bowl. Beat in egg yolks and almond extract. Add flour and baking powder, beating until combined.
3. Using a 1-tablespoon (about 17 grams) spring-loaded scoop, scoop dough, and roll into 1-inch balls. Place 2 inches apart on prepared pans. Using your thumb or the back of a small spoon, make an indentation in center of each ball. Freeze until firm, about 20 minutes.
4. Preheat oven to 350°F (180°C).
5. Bake until bottoms are golden brown, 14 to 16 minutes. Press down centers again. Let cool on pans for 5 minutes. Remove from pans, and let cool completely on wire racks.
6. In a small bowl, whisk together 1 tablespoon (15 grams) water and remaining ½ cup (60 grams) confectioners' sugar until smooth.
7. Just before serving, spoon ½ teaspoon (3 grams) Quick Cranberry Jam into center of each cooled cookie. Drizzle with glaze, and garnish with orange zest, if desired. Refrigerate in an airtight container for up to 3 days.

Quick Cranberry Jam

Makes about ½ cup

- ¾ cup (100 grams) fresh or drained thawed frozen cranberries
- ¼ cup (50 grams) granulated sugar
- 3 tablespoons (45 grams) water
- ½ teaspoon (1 gram) orange zest

1. In a medium saucepan, bring cranberries, sugar, 3 tablespoons (45 grams) water, and orange zest to a boil over medium-high heat. Reduce heat to medium, and cook until thickened, about 6 minutes. Using the edge of a spatula, mash cranberries. Remove from heat, and let cool completely. Refrigerate in an airtight container for up to 1 week.

PB&J Cookies

Makes about 15 cookies

Chewy honey- and brown sugar-sweetened peanut butter cookies get a simple filling of fruity jelly before being rolled in turbinado sugar and baked to golden perfection. They're a PB&J lover's dream.

- ½ cup (113 grams) unsalted butter, softened
- 1 cup (220 grams) firmly packed light brown sugar
- 1 large egg (50 grams), room temperature
- 2 large egg yolks (37 grams), room temperature
- ¾ cup (192 grams) creamy peanut butter
- 1 tablespoon (21 grams) honey
- 1 teaspoon (4 grams) vanilla extract
- 2¼ cups (281 grams) all-purpose flour
- 1 teaspoon (5 grams) baking powder
- ¼ teaspoon (1.25 grams) baking soda
- ¾ cup (240 grams) grape jelly
- ½ cup (100 grams) turbinado sugar

NOTE: *Work one at a time so the jelly doesn't slide when you aren't looking. Place the jelly-sandwiched disks in your hand to crimp and use your palm to cup the sides and shape them so they're smooth and rounded to lessen cracking. Use any flavor of jelly you like.*

1. In the bowl of a stand mixer fitted with the paddle attachment, beat butter and brown sugar at medium speed until fluffy, 3 to 4 minutes, stopping to scrape sides of bowl. Add egg and egg yolks, beating until well combined. Beat in peanut butter, honey, and vanilla.

2. In a large bowl, whisk together flour, baking powder, and baking soda. With mixer on low speed, gradually add flour mixture to butter mixture, beating just until combined. Cover and refrigerate for at least 1 hour.

3. Preheat oven to 325°F (170°C). Line baking sheets with parchment paper.

4. Using a 1½-tablespoon (about 30 grams) spring-loaded scoop, scoop dough, roll into balls, and flatten into 2½-inch disks. Spoon 2 teaspoons (14 grams) jelly into center of 1 dough disk, and cover with a second disk. Crimp edges to seal, and gently shape edges to be smooth and rounded. (See Note.) Repeat with remaining jelly and remaining dough disks. Place 2 inches apart on prepared pans. Sprinkle with turbinado sugar, lightly pressing into tops.

5. Bake until bottoms are golden brown and tops look dry, 14 to 16 minutes, rotating pans halfway through baking. Let cool completely on pans on wire racks. Store in an airtight container for up to 3 days.

Carrot Cake Sandwich Cookies

Makes 22 sandwich cookies

I kept the base flavors of these tender cookies faithful to the original, with a carrot-rich dough brimming with pecans. A thick layer of Sour Cream Buttercream adds the perfect amount of tang to every bite.

- 1 cup (227 grams) unsalted butter, softened
- 1¼ cups (275 grams) firmly packed dark brown sugar
- ½ cup (100 grams) granulated sugar
- 2 large eggs (100 grams), room temperature
- 2 teaspoons (8 grams) vanilla extract
- 2¾ cups (344 grams) all-purpose flour
- 1½ teaspoons (3 grams) ground cinnamon
- 1 teaspoon (3 grams) kosher salt
- ¾ teaspoon (3.75 grams) baking soda
- ½ teaspoon (1 gram) ground allspice
- ½ teaspoon (1 gram) ground ginger
- 1½ cups (120 grams) old-fashioned oats
- 1 cup (107 grams) lightly packed grated carrots
- ½ cup (57 grams) finely chopped pecans
- Sour Cream Buttercream (recipe follows)

1. Preheat oven to 350°F (180°C). Line baking sheets with parchment paper.

2. In the bowl of a stand mixer fitted with the paddle attachment, beat butter and sugars at medium speed until fluffy, 3 to 4 minutes, stopping to scrape sides of bowl. Add eggs, one at a time, beating well after each addition. Beat in vanilla.

3. In a medium bowl, whisk together flour, cinnamon, salt, baking soda, allspice, and ginger. With mixer on low speed, gradually add flour mixture to butter mixture, beating just until combined. Beat in oats, carrot, and pecans. Using a 1½-tablespoon (about 28 grams) scoop, scoop dough. Using floured hands, roll each dough scoop into a smooth ball; press into a disk (2 inches in diameter and ⅝ inch thick). Place 2 inches apart on prepared pans.

4. Bake until edges are golden brown, 11 to 14 minutes. Let cool on pans for 5 minutes. Remove from pans, and let cool completely on wire racks.

5. Place Sour Cream Buttercream in a pastry bag fitted with ½-inch round piping tip (Wilton 1A). Pipe a large dollop of buttercream onto flat side of half of cookies, leaving a ¼-inch border. Place remaining cookies, flat side down, on top of buttercream, gently pressing to push buttercream to edges of cookies. Refrigerate in an airtight container for up to 3 days. Let stand at room temperature for 10 to 15 minutes before serving.

Sour Cream Buttercream

Makes about 2½ cups

- ½ cup (113 grams) unsalted butter, softened
- ½ cup (120 grams) sour cream
- ½ teaspoon (2 grams) vanilla extract
- ¼ teaspoon kosher salt
- 3 cups (360 grams) confectioners' sugar

1. In the bowl of a stand mixer fitted with the paddle attachment, beat butter at medium speed until smooth, about 1 minute. Add half of sour cream, vanilla, and salt; beat at low speed just until combined. Add half of confectioners' sugar, beating until combined. Beat in remaining sour cream. Add remaining confectioners' sugar, and beat at medium speed until smooth and fluffy, stopping to scrape paddle and bottom and sides of bowl. Use immediately.

Pineapple-Ginger Thumbprint Cookies

Makes about 50 cookies

I reimagined the classic Southeast Asian pineapple tart as a zingy ginger cookie topped with spiced, caramelized pineapple jam. As a nod to the original's elegant stamped shape, I like to pipe these cookies into a mesmerizing swirl.

---

1 cup (227 grams) unsalted butter, softened
⅔ cup (133 grams) granulated sugar
1 large egg (50 grams)
1 teaspoon (3 grams) finely grated fresh ginger
1 teaspoon (4 grams) vanilla extract
2⅔ cups (333 grams) all-purpose flour
1 teaspoon (2 grams) ground ginger
¾ teaspoon (2.25 grams) kosher salt
¼ teaspoon (1.25 grams) baking powder
Pineapple Jam Filling (recipe follows)

1. Preheat oven to 350°F (180°C). Line baking sheets with parchment paper.
2. In the bowl of a stand mixer fitted with the paddle attachment, beat butter and sugar at medium speed until creamy, 2 to 3 minutes, stopping to scrape sides of bowl. Add egg, beating well. Beat in fresh ginger and vanilla.
3. In a medium bowl, whisk together flour, ground ginger, salt, and baking powder. With mixer on low speed, gradually add flour mixture to butter mixture, beating until combined.
4. Transfer about ½ cup dough to a pastry bag fitted with a medium open star piping tip (Wilton 1M). Pipe 1½-inch rosettes 3 inches apart on prepared pans, pinching dough with fingers to release. (Spacing these cookies farther apart ensures even heating during baking for better shape.) Repeat with remaining dough, ½ cup at a time.
5. Bake for 5 minutes. Using the handle of a wooden spoon, gently make an indentation in center of each cookie. Top each with Pineapple Jam Filling. Bake until cookies are lightly browned, 6 to 8 minutes more. Let cool on pans for 10 minutes. Remove from pans, and let cool completely on wire racks. Refrigerate in an airtight container for up to 3 days.

Pineapple Jam Filling

Makes about 1½ cups

2 medium pineapples, peeled, cored, and cubed (about 2¼ pounds)
1 cinnamon stick
½ teaspoon (1 gram) whole cloves
½ cup (100 grams) granulated sugar
1 tablespoon (15 grams) fresh lemon juice

1. In the work bowl of a food processor, pulse pineapple until puréed. Transfer pineapple purée to a large skillet. Add cinnamon stick and cloves; cook over medium heat, stirring frequently, until most of liquid is evaporated, about 15 minutes. Stir in sugar and lemon juice; increase heat to medium-high. Bring to a boil; cook, stirring frequently to reduce spattering, for 5 minutes. Reduce heat; simmer, stirring frequently to prevent scorching, until thick and golden in color, about 40 minutes.
2. Transfer pineapple mixture to a bowl. Let cool for 30 minutes. Discard cinnamon stick and cloves. Cover and refrigerate for at least 1 hour.
3. Line a baking sheet with parchment paper. Scoop pineapple mixture by teaspoonfuls (about 7 grams), and shape into balls. Place on prepared pan until ready to use.

Wedding Cake Sandwich Cookies

Makes 15 sandwich cookies

As a child, I loved weddings and went to as many as I could. My mom was a church organist, my aunt Janice was a wedding coordinator, and my aunt Cheryl loved a good slice of cake. As I grew up and realized I was gay, my love for weddings faded. How could I love something I wouldn't be able to have myself? It saddened me to think that I wouldn't be able to celebrate my future love and my future husband along with my own wedding cake, so I became comfortable on team "I don't need a wedding to be in love, so I don't want one." Then I met Stephen. And I wanted one. After a trip to Seattle, Washington, to get legally married in the courthouse (this was 2013, two years before the nationwide ruling), we had our dream wedding at my mom's house in Alabama on a bluff at sunset, surrounded by 150 people who love us—complete with my dream wedding cake. This recipe is the flavor of that cake, with rainbow sprinkles added. Now, a celebration is never too far from reach.

- **1 cup (227 grams) unsalted butter, softened**
- **2 cups (400 grams) granulated sugar, divided**
- **2 large eggs (100 grams), room temperature**
- **1 tablespoon (18 grams) vanilla bean paste or 1 tablespoon (13 grams) vanilla extract**
- **½ teaspoon (2 grams) almond extract**
- **2¼ cups (281 grams) all-purpose flour**
- **¾ cup (95 grams) bread flour**
- **2 teaspoons (10 grams) baking powder**
- **2 teaspoons (6 grams) cream of tartar**
- **1 teaspoon (5 grams) baking soda**
- **1 teaspoon (3 grams) kosher salt**
- **2 tablespoons (30 grams) whole milk**
- **1 cup (180 grams) rainbow sprinkles, plus more for topping**
- **Wedding Cake Buttercream (recipe follows)**

1. In the bowl of a stand mixer fitted with the paddle attachment, beat butter and 1⅓ cups sugar (267 grams) at medium speed until fluffy, 3 to 4 minutes, stopping to scrape sides of bowl. Add eggs, one at a time, beating well after each addition. Beat in vanilla paste or extract and almond extract.
2. In a medium bowl, whisk together flours, baking powder, cream of tartar, baking soda, and salt. With mixer on low speed, gradually add flour mixture to butter mixture, beating just until combined. Add milk; beat until combined. Fold in sprinkles. Cover bowl with plastic wrap, and refrigerate for at least 1 hour or up to 3 days.
3. Preheat oven to 350°F (180°C). Line baking sheets with parchment paper.
4. Using a 1½-inch spring-loaded scoop, scoop dough, and roll into balls. Roll balls in remaining ⅔ cup (133 grams) sugar. Place 3 inches apart on prepared pans; top with more sprinkles, if desired.
5. Bake until edges are lightly browned, 12 to 14 minutes. Let cool on pans for 5 minutes. Remove from pans, and let cool completely on wire racks.
6. Place Wedding Cake Buttercream in a pastry bag fitted with a large star piping tip (Ateco #825). Pipe buttercream onto flat side of half of cookies. Place remaining cookies, flat side down, on top of buttercream. Store in an airtight container for up to 3 days.

Wedding Cake Buttercream

Makes about 2 cups

- **¼ cup (57 grams) unsalted butter, softened**
- **3¾ cups (450 grams) confectioners' sugar, sifted**
- **¼ cup (60 grams) whole milk**
- **¼ teaspoon (1 gram) almond extract**

1. In the bowl of a stand mixer fitted with the paddle attachment, beat butter at medium speed until creamy. With mixer on low speed, gradually add confectioners' sugar and milk, beating until smooth and well combined, stopping to scrape paddle and bottom and sides of bowl. Add almond extract, and beat until light and fluffy. Use immediately.

Apple Cider Whoopie Pies

Makes 9 whoopie pies

There are few bakes that'll satisfy cozy cravings quite like these Apple Cider Whoopie Pies. For my twist on the Northeastern favorite, tender apple-and-spice cookies are brushed with butter and dipped in a sparkly spiced sugar before being sandwiched with luscious Cream Cheese Buttercream. Don't forget your mug of hot cider to enjoy alongside them.

¾ cup (170 grams) unsalted butter, softened
¾ cup (165 grams) firmly packed light brown sugar
1 large egg (50 grams), room temperature
3 cups (375 grams) all-purpose flour
1 tablespoon (6 grams) plus ¾ teaspoon (1.5 grams) apple pie spice, divided
2 teaspoons (10 grams) baking powder
½ teaspoon (2.5 grams) baking soda
½ teaspoon (1.5 grams) kosher salt
½ cup (160 grams) Boiled Cider (recipe follows)
¾ cup (150 grams) granulated sugar
1 tablespoon (14 grams) unsalted butter, melted
Cream Cheese Buttercream (recipe on opposite page)

1. Preheat oven to 350°F (180°C). Line baking sheets with parchment paper.
2. In the bowl of a stand mixer fitted with the paddle attachment, beat butter and brown sugar at medium speed until creamy, 3 to 4 minutes, stopping to scrape sides of bowl. Beat in egg until combined.
3. In a medium bowl, whisk together flour, 1 tablespoon (6 grams) pie spice, baking powder, baking soda, and salt. With mixer on low speed, gradually add flour mixture to butter mixture alternately with Boiled Cider, beginning and ending with flour mixture, beating just until combined after each addition and stopping to scrape sides of bowl. (Batter will be thick.) Using a 3-tablespoon spring-loaded scoop, scoop batter level, and place at least 2 inches apart on prepared pans.
4. Bake until bottom edges are lightly golden and tops are dry, 12 to 14 minutes, rotating pans halfway through baking. Let cool completely on pans.
5. In a small bowl, stir together granulated sugar and remaining ¾ teaspoon (1.5 grams) pie spice.
6. Working with 1 at a time, lightly brush top and edges of each cookie with melted butter. Place, top side down, in sugar mixture, making sure top and edges are coated. Place back on pans. (Sprinkle remaining sugar mixture on tops as needed for any areas where there might have been too much butter.)
7. Place Cream Cheese Buttercream in a pastry bag fitted with a ½-inch round piping tip (Ateco #807). Pipe buttercream onto flat side of half of cookies. Place remaining cookies, flat side down, on buttercream. Serve immediately, or refrigerate in an airtight container for up to 5 days.

Boiled Cider

Makes 1 cup

8 cups (1,956 grams) apple cider

1. In a large saucepan, bring cider to a boil over medium-high heat; cook, checking frequently, until cider is the consistency of maple syrup and reduced to 1 cup, 1 hour to 1 hour and 20 minutes. Pour mixture into a heatproof liquid-measuring cup; let cool completely before measuring and using. (If not using the same day, cover and refrigerate; let come to room temperature before using.)

Make Ahead

Boiled Cider can be made well in advance and refrigerated in an airtight container for up to 3 months. This recipe makes enough for a double batch of whoopie pies. You can also stir the extra in cocktails or tea, drizzle onto ice cream and desserts, or swirl into yogurt or oatmeal for breakfast.

Cream Cheese Buttercream

Makes 3 cups

- ½ cup (113 grams) unsalted butter, softened
- 1 (8-ounce) package (226 grams) cream cheese, softened
- 4 cups (480 grams) confectioners' sugar
- ½ teaspoon (2 grams) vanilla extract

1. In the bowl of a stand mixer fitted with the paddle attachment, beat butter at medium speed until smooth, about 1 minute. Add cream cheese, and beat until smooth and combined, stopping to scrape paddle and bottom and sides of bowl. With mixer on low speed, gradually add confectioners' sugar, beating until just combined. Beat in vanilla; increase mixer speed to medium, and beat until light and fluffy, about 30 seconds.

Cream-Filled Basque Cookies

Makes about 18 cookies

These indulgent cream-filled cookies embody the flavors of the gâteau Basque, which is a buttery cake with a pastry cream filling that originates from the Basque region in southwestern France. I added crème fraîche to the cookie dough for a tanginess that perfectly complements its vanilla-rich sweetness.

- ½ cup (113 grams) unsalted butter, softened
- 1 cup (200 grams) granulated sugar
- 2 large eggs (100 grams)
- 1 vanilla bean, split lengthwise, seeds scraped and reserved
- 2½ cups (313 grams) all-purpose flour, plus more for dusting
- ½ teaspoon (2.5 grams) baking powder
- ½ teaspoon (2.5 grams) baking soda
- ½ teaspoon (1.5 grams) kosher salt
- ⅓ cup plus 2 tablespoons (110 grams) crème fraîche
- Vanilla Pastry Cream (recipe follows)

1. In the bowl of a stand mixer fitted with the paddle attachment, beat butter and sugar at medium speed until fluffy, 3 to 4 minutes, stopping to scrape sides of bowl. Add eggs, one at a time, beating well after each addition. Beat in reserved vanilla seeds.
2. In a medium bowl, whisk together flour, baking powder, baking soda, and salt. With mixer on low speed, gradually add flour mixture to butter mixture alternately with crème fraîche, beginning and ending with flour mixture, beating just until combined after each addition.
3. Divide dough in half. Roll each half between 2 sheets of parchment paper to ⅛-inch thickness. Transfer dough between parchment to refrigerator. Refrigerate overnight.
4. Preheat oven to 375°F (190°C). Line rimmed baking sheets with parchment paper.
5. Using a 2-inch round cutter, cut half of dough. Using a 3-inch round cutter, cut remaining dough. With floured hands, place a 3-inch round in your palm. Place 1 tablespoon chilled Vanilla Pastry Cream in center. Top with a 2-inch round; fold edges together and under, and pinch edges to seal. (If dough is too soft to handle, freeze for 10 to 15 minutes to firm up.) Using your finger, brush edges with water if there is too much flour. Place cookies, seam side down, at least 2 inches apart on prepared pans. Repeat with remaining dough, rerolling scraps as necessary.
6. Bake until bottom edges are golden and tops look dry, 8 to 10 minutes. Let cool on pans for 2 minutes. Remove from pans, and let cool completely on wire racks. Store in an airtight container for up to 3 days.

Vanilla Pastry Cream

Makes about 1¾ cups

- 1½ cups (360 grams) whole milk
- ½ cup (100 grams) granulated sugar, divided
- 1 vanilla bean, split lengthwise, seeds scraped and reserved
- 4 large egg yolks (74 grams)
- 3½ tablespoons (28 grams) cornstarch
- ¼ teaspoon kosher salt
- 2 tablespoons (28 grams) unsalted butter, softened

1. In a large saucepan, whisk together milk, ¼ cup (50 grams) sugar, and vanilla bean and reserved seeds. Heat over medium heat until steaming. (Do not boil.) Discard vanilla bean.
2. In a large bowl, whisk together egg yolks, cornstarch, salt, and remaining ¼ cup (50 grams) sugar. Gradually add warm milk mixture, whisking constantly. Pour egg yolk mixture into saucepan, and cook over medium heat, whisking constantly, until thickened and boiling, 4 to 5 minutes. Strain mixture through a fine-mesh sieve into a large bowl. Stir in butter in two additions. Cover with plastic wrap, pressing wrap directly onto surface of pastry cream to prevent a skin from forming. Refrigerate until completely chilled, about 4 hours, or overnight.

Oatmeal Sandwich Cookies

Makes about 22 sandwich cookies

Do you remember opening those crinkly plastic wrappers and getting hit with the sweet, oat-y smell of pillowy-soft cookies and sugary frosting? Well, these are all that and more. The cookies are slightly crisp on the outside and perfectly chewy on the inside, making them perfect for sandwiching together with a generous slathering of buttercream.

- 3 cups (300 grams) old-fashioned oats
- ½ cup (80 grams) roughly chopped raisins
- 2 cups (250 grams) all-purpose flour
- 2 tablespoons (10 grams) unsweetened cocoa powder
- 1½ teaspoons (4.5 grams) kosher salt
- 1 teaspoon (2 grams) ground cinnamon
- ½ teaspoon (2.5 grams) baking soda
- ¼ teaspoon (1.25 grams) baking powder
- 1 cup (227 grams) unsalted butter, softened
- 1¾ cups (385 grams) firmly packed light brown sugar
- 2 large eggs (100 grams), room temperature
- 2 tablespoons (42 grams) molasses
- 1 teaspoon (4 grams) vanilla extract
- Vanilla Buttercream (recipe follows)

1. In the work bowl of a food processor, pulse oats until uniform in size and almost ground but not too powdery. Add raisins, and pulse until raisins are finely chopped. Add flour, cocoa, salt, cinnamon, baking soda, and baking powder; pulse just until combined.
2. In the bowl of a stand mixer fitted with the paddle attachment, beat butter and brown sugar at medium speed until fluffy, 2 to 3 minutes, stopping to scrape sides of bowl. Add eggs, one at a time, beating well after each addition. Beat in molasses and vanilla until combined. With mixer on low speed, add oats mixture in two additions, beating until combined after each addition. Cover and refrigerate for 30 minutes.
3. Preheat oven to 350°F (180°C). Line baking sheets with parchment paper.
4. Using a 1½-tablespoon (about 30 grams) spring-loaded scoop, scoop dough, and roll into smooth balls. Place 2 inches apart on prepared pans.
5. Bake until bottom edges are golden but centers look a little wet, 8 to 12 minutes. (Do not overbake.) Let cool on pans for 5 minutes. Remove from pans, and let cool completely on wire racks.
6. Place Vanilla Buttercream in a pastry bag fitted with a ½-inch round piping tip. Pipe buttercream onto flat side of half of cookies. Place remaining cookies, flat side down, on top of buttercream. Store in an airtight container for up to 3 days.

Vanilla Buttercream

Makes about 2½ cups

- 1 cup (227 grams) unsalted butter, softened
- 1 teaspoon (6 grams) vanilla bean paste
- ¼ teaspoon kosher salt
- 4 cups (480 grams) confectioners' sugar
- 1 tablespoon (15 grams) whole milk

1. In the bowl of a stand mixer fitted with the paddle attachment, beat butter, vanilla bean paste, and salt at medium speed until smooth and well combined. Reduce mixer speed to low; gradually add half of confectioners' sugar, beating until smooth. Beat in milk until combined; scrape sides of bowl. Add remaining confectioners' sugar, and beat until smooth and well combined.

Chocolate-Cherry Browned Butter Sandwich Cookies with Whiskey Buttercream

Makes 16 sandwich cookies

These cookies are jam-packed with chocolate as well as dried tart cherries cooked in Irish whiskey, and I didn't stop there—there's also Irish whiskey and browned butter in the frosting.

1¼ cups (283 grams) unsalted butter, cubed
½ cup (115 grams) packed dried tart cherries, chopped
¼ cup (52 grams) plus 1½ teaspoons (6.5 grams) Irish whiskey, divided
⅔ cup (133 grams) granulated sugar
⅔ cup (147 grams) firmly packed light brown sugar
1 large egg (50 grams), room temperature
½ teaspoon (2 grams) vanilla extract
1¾ cups (219 grams) all-purpose flour
2 tablespoons (16 grams) cornstarch
1 teaspoon (3 grams) kosher salt
½ teaspoon (2.5 grams) baking powder
½ teaspoon (2.5 grams) baking soda
½ cup (85 grams) chopped dark chocolate
Whiskey Buttercream (recipe on opposite page)

NOTE: *Gram weights of browned butter may vary slightly depending on the brand of butter used.*

1. In a medium saucepan, melt butter over medium heat. Cook, stirring frequently, until butter solids are golden and nutty in aroma, 7 to 12 minutes. Pour ¾ cup (139 grams) browned butter into a medium shallow bowl. Pour remaining ½ cup (94 grams) browned butter into another medium shallow bowl, reserving for Whiskey Buttercream. (See Note.) Refrigerate both until browned butter is solid, 2 to 3 hours. Let stand at room temperature until softened before using, about 30 minutes.
2. In a small microwave-safe bowl, combine cherries and ¼ cup (52 grams) whiskey; heat on high until hot, about 2 minutes. Let stand for at least 30 minutes, stirring occasionally. Drain cherries.
3. In the bowl of a stand mixer fitted with the paddle attachment, beat ¾ cup (139 grams) browned butter at medium speed until creamy, 30 seconds to 1 minute; scrape sides of bowl. Add sugars, and beat until fluffy, about 2 minutes, stopping to scrape sides of bowl. Beat in egg, vanilla, and remaining 1½ teaspoons (6.5 grams) whiskey until well combined.
4. In a medium bowl, whisk together flour, cornstarch, salt, baking powder, and baking soda. Add flour mixture to butter mixture, and beat at low speed just until combined. Fold in cherries and chocolate. Cover and refrigerate for 1 hour.
5. Preheat oven to 350°F (180°C). Line rimmed baking sheets with parchment paper.
6. Using a 1½-tablespoon (about 28 grams) spring-loaded scoop, scoop dough, and roll into balls. Place 2 inches apart on prepared pans.
7. Bake until light golden brown, about 10 minutes. (Cookies may still seem slightly underdone in centers but will set up as they cool; warm cookies can be formed right out of the oven into a more circular shape, if desired. Using an offset spatula, gently press and curve uneven edges of still-warm cookies.) Let cool on pans for 5 minutes. Remove from pans, and let cool completely on wire racks.
8. Spoon Whiskey Buttercream into a large pastry bag fitted with a medium open star piping tip (Wilton 1M). Pipe buttercream onto flat side of half of cookies. Place remaining cookies, flat side down, on top of buttercream. Store in an airtight container for up to 3 days.

Whiskey Buttercream

Makes 2 cups

- ½ cup (94 grams) browned butter (reserved from step 1 of cookies), softened
- ¼ teaspoon kosher salt
- 3½ tablespoons (45.5 grams) Irish whiskey
- 2 tablespoons (30 grams) heavy whipping cream
- 4 cups (480 grams) confectioners' sugar, sifted

1. In the bowl of a stand mixer fitted with the paddle attachment, beat browned butter and salt at medium speed until creamy, 30 seconds to 1 minute; scrape sides of bowl.
2. In a small bowl, whisk together whiskey and cream.
3. With mixer on low speed, gradually add confectioners' sugar to butter mixture alternately with whiskey mixture, beginning and ending with confectioners' sugar, beating just until combined after each addition and stopping to scrape sides of bowl. Increase mixer speed to medium, and beat until fluffy, about 2 minutes, stopping to scrape paddle and bottom and sides of bowl. Use immediately.

Black Cocoa Sandwich Cookies

Makes about 13 sandwich cookies

These are just like Oreo sandwich cookies—only bigger, better, and completely from scratch.

- **¼ cup plus 3 tablespoons (36 grams) black cocoa powder (see Note)**
- **3 tablespoons (42 grams) unsalted butter, melted**
- **5 tablespoons (70 grams) unsalted butter, softened**
- **½ cup (110 grams) firmly packed light brown sugar**
- **¼ teaspoon kosher salt**
- **1 large egg (50 grams)**
- **1 teaspoon (4 grams) vanilla extract**
- **1½ cups (188 grams) all-purpose flour**
- **Vanilla Filling (recipe follows)**

NOTE: *Black cocoa powder is not the same as dark, Dutch process, or unsweetened cocoa powders. Black cocoa powder is readily available online.*

1. In a small bowl, whisk together cocoa and melted butter. Let cool slightly.
2. In the bowl of a stand mixer fitted with the paddle attachment, beat softened butter, brown sugar, and salt at medium speed until fluffy, 3 to 4 minutes, stopping to scrape sides of bowl. Beat in cocoa mixture. Add egg and vanilla, beating until well combined. Add flour, and beat until fully incorporated and a smooth dough forms. Shape dough into a disk, and wrap in plastic wrap. Refrigerate for at least 1 hour.
3. Preheat oven to 325°F (170°C).
4. Place dough between 2 sheets of parchment paper, and roll dough to ⅛-inch thickness. Using a 3-inch fluted round cutter, cut dough. Remove dough scraps, leaving cutout dough on parchment. Place dough on parchment on a baking sheet. Repeat rolling and cutting procedure with scraps to use all dough. (If dough gets too soft to roll, freeze for 5 to 10 minutes to firm.)
5. Bake until a slight indentation is left when pressed with a finger, about 10 minutes. Let cool completely on pans on wire racks.
6. Place Vanilla Filling in a pastry bag fitted with a medium round piping tip. Pipe filling onto flat side of half of cookies. Place remaining cookies, flat side down, on top of filling. Store in an airtight container for up to 3 days.

Vanilla Filling

Makes about 2 cups

- **1 cup (227 grams) unsalted butter, softened**
- **4 cups (480 grams) confectioners' sugar**
- **1 teaspoon (6 grams) vanilla bean paste**
- **⅛ teaspoon kosher salt**

1. In the bowl of a stand mixer fitted with the paddle attachment, beat butter at medium speed until creamy, 5 to 6 minutes. Gradually add confectioners' sugar, beating until combined. Add vanilla bean paste and salt, beating until smooth.

Custard Crèmes

Makes 13 sandwich cookies

In the United Kingdom, these cookies are as beloved as Little Debbie Oatmeal Creme Pies or Oreos are in the United States. One bite of these and you'll understand the fanfare. Custard powder makes the buttery shortbread dough and filling even richer.

---

1 cup (227 grams) unsalted butter, softened
⅔ cup (133 grams) granulated sugar
1 teaspoon (4 grams) vanilla extract
¾ teaspoon (2.25 grams) kosher salt
2⅓ cups (292 grams) all-purpose flour, plus more for dusting
½ cup (65 grams) custard powder
Custard Buttercream (recipe follows)

1. In the bowl of a stand mixer fitted with the paddle attachment, beat butter, sugar, vanilla, and salt at medium speed until creamy, 2 to 3 minutes, stopping to scrape sides of bowl.
2. In a medium bowl, whisk together flour and custard powder. With mixer on low speed, gradually add flour mixture to butter mixture, beating until dough begins to clump together. Turn out dough onto a lightly floured surface, and shape into a disk. Wrap in plastic wrap, and refrigerate until chilled, about 1 hour.
3. Preheat oven to 350°F (180°C). Line baking sheets with parchment paper.
4. On a lightly floured surface, roll dough to ⅛-inch thickness. Using your desired cookie stamp dipped in flour, firmly press pattern into dough. Using a 3-inch fluted round cutter, cut dough, rerolling scraps to use all dough, and place 1 inch apart on prepared pans. (Work quickly so dough does not get warm and sticky.) Freeze until firm, about 10 minutes.
5. Bake until edges are beginning to brown, 10 to 12 minutes. Let cool on pans for 10 minutes. Remove from pans, and let cool completely on wire racks.
6. Spoon Custard Buttercream into a pastry bag; cut a ¾-inch opening in tip. Pipe 2 tablespoons (26 grams) buttercream onto flat side of half of cookies. Place remaining cookies, flat side down, on buttercream. Store in an airtight container for up to 3 days.

Custard Buttercream

Makes 2 cups

¾ cup (170 grams) unsalted butter, softened
⅛ teaspoon kosher salt
¼ cup (33 grams) custard powder
1 teaspoon (6 grams) vanilla bean paste
2 cups (240 grams) confectioners' sugar
1 tablespoon (15 grams) heavy whipping cream

1. In the bowl of a stand mixer fitted with the paddle attachment, beat butter and salt at medium speed until smooth, 2 to 3 minutes. Beat in custard powder and vanilla bean paste. With mixer on low speed, gradually add confectioners' sugar, beating until combined. Add cream; increase mixer speed to medium-high, and beat until light and airy, 1 to 2 minutes. Use immediately.

Cookie Butter-Stuffed Snickerdoodles

Makes about 26 cookies

Cookie butter is a delicious spread made from speculaas, a type of spiced shortcrust cookie that's similar to a graham cracker or a crunchy gingersnap, and it's easily located with the jams and spreads in your favorite grocery store. Cookie butter works great with the caramelly sweet and spice of a snickerdoodle.

- 1 (14.1-ounce) jar (400 grams) cookie butter
- 1 cup (227 grams) unsalted butter, softened
- 1½ cups (300 grams) granulated sugar, divided
- ½ cup (110 grams) firmly packed light brown sugar
- 2 large eggs (100 grams), room temperature
- 1½ teaspoons (6 grams) vanilla extract
- 2¾ cups (344 grams) all-purpose flour
- 1½ teaspoons (4.5 grams) cream of tartar
- 1 teaspoon (3 grams) kosher salt
- ½ teaspoon (2.5 grams) baking soda
- 2½ teaspoons (5 grams) ground cinnamon
- Cookie Butter Glaze (recipe follows)
- Speculaas cookie crumbs, for sprinkling

1. Line baking sheets with parchment paper.
2. Using a 1-tablespoon spring-loaded scoop, scoop cookie butter (about 15 grams each), and place on a prepared pan; freeze until solid, about 1 hour.
3. In the bowl of a stand mixer fitted with the paddle attachment, beat butter, 1 cup (200 grams) granulated sugar, and brown sugar at medium speed until fluffy, 3 to 4 minutes, stopping to scrape sides of bowl. Add eggs, one at a time, beating well after each addition. Beat in vanilla.
4. In a medium bowl, whisk together flour, cream of tartar, salt, and baking soda. With mixer on low speed, gradually add flour mixture to butter mixture, beating just until combined.
5. Using a 1-tablespoon (about 17 grams) spring-loaded scoop, scoop dough, and gently flatten each with the palm of your hand. Place 1 portion of frozen cookie butter on 1 flattened dough scoop; top with another flattened dough scoop. Press edges together to seal. Roll into a 1½-inch ball; place on a prepared pan. Repeat with remaining dough and remaining frozen cookie butter. Freeze until firm, about 10 minutes.
6. Preheat oven to 375°F (190°C).
7. In another medium bowl, whisk together cinnamon and remaining ½ cup (100 grams) granulated sugar. Toss dough balls in cinnamon sugar until well coated. Place 2 inches apart on prepared pans.
8. Bake, one pan at a time, until edges are lightly browned and centers look slightly wet, 7 to 10 minutes. Let cool on pans for 5 minutes. Remove from pans, and let cool completely on wire racks.
9. Drizzle Cookie Butter Glaze onto cooled cookies; sprinkle with cookie crumbs. Store in an airtight container for up to 3 days.

Cookie Butter Glaze

Makes about 1 cup

- 1 cup (120 grams) confectioners' sugar
- 3 tablespoons plus 2 teaspoons (55 grams) heavy whipping cream
- 2 tablespoons (30 grams) cookie butter

1. In a small bowl, whisk together all ingredients until smooth. Use immediately.

Peanut Butter Brownie Cookie Cups

Makes 12 cookie cups

Flourless chocolate cake meets peanut butter cookies in this makeover that packs both fudgy and crunchy textures into one perfect bite.

- **4 ounces (113 grams) bittersweet chocolate, chopped**
- **½ cup (113 grams) unsalted butter, cubed**
- **¾ cup (192 grams) creamy peanut butter, divided**
- **3 large eggs (150 grams), room temperature**
- **¾ cup (150 grams) granulated sugar**
- **¼ teaspoon kosher salt**
- **½ teaspoon (2 grams) vanilla extract**
- **½ cup (43 grams) Dutch process cocoa powder, sifted**
- **Cookie Crust (recipe follows)**
- **½ cup (120 grams) whole milk**

NOTE: *The peanut butter drizzle acts kind of like a ganache when heating. You're looking for a smooth, emulsified mixture. If it is not consistently shiny or it looks slightly broken, continue heating in 10-second intervals.*

1. Preheat oven to 325°F (170°C). Spray a 12-cup muffin pan with cooking spray.
2. In the top of a double boiler, combine chocolate, butter, and ¼ cup (64 grams) peanut butter. Cook over simmering water, stirring occasionally, until melted and smooth. Remove from heat. Let cool for 10 minutes.
3. In a large bowl, beat eggs with a handheld mixer at medium speed until foamy. Add sugar and salt in a slow, steady stream, beating until pale yellow, about 2 minutes. Fold in chocolate mixture and vanilla until combined. Fold in cocoa.
4. Press 2 tablespoons (38 grams) Cookie Crust into bottom and up sides of each prepared muffin cup. Divide batter among prepared crusts (about 3 tablespoons or 50 grams each).
5. Bake until tops are dry and a wooden pick inserted in center comes out with a few moist crumbs, 15 to 20 minutes. Let cool in pan for 10 minutes. Remove from pan, and let cool completely on a wire rack. (Centers will fall as they cool.)
6. In a small microwave-safe bowl, heat milk and remaining ½ cup (128 grams) peanut butter on high in 10-second intervals, stirring between each, until peanut butter is melted and mixture is smooth. Drizzle glaze onto cooled cookie cups; let stand until set, about 10 minutes. Store in an airtight container for up to 3 days.

Cookie Crust

Makes 1½ cups

- **⅔ cup (150 grams) unsalted butter, softened**
- **⅓ cup (73 grams) firmly packed dark brown sugar**
- **1 large egg yolk (19 grams), room temperature**
- **1 teaspoon (4 grams) vanilla extract**
- **1¾ cups (219 grams) whole wheat flour**
- **1 teaspoon (3 grams) kosher salt**

1. In the bowl of a stand mixer fitted with the paddle attachment, beat butter and brown sugar at medium-low speed until creamy, about 3 minutes, stopping to scrape sides of bowl. Add egg yolk and vanilla, and beat at medium speed until smooth, about 2 minutes. Add flour and salt, and beat at low speed just until combined and dough holds together when pressed.

Chocolate-Covered Marshmallow Cookies

Makes 20 cookies

A homemade take on the classic Mallomar, these cookies layer crisp, spiced gingersnaps with a fluffy Swiss meringue-style marshmallow enrobed in a glossy dark chocolate shell.

- 2 large egg whites (60 grams), room temperature
- ¾ cup (255 grams) light corn syrup
- ⅓ cup (67 grams) granulated sugar
- ½ teaspoon (1.5 grams) kosher salt
- ½ teaspoon (1 gram) cream of tartar
- 1½ teaspoons (6 grams) vanilla extract
- 20 Gingersnaps (recipe follows)
- 10 ounces (300 grams) dark chocolate melting wafers

1. Line a rimmed baking sheet with parchment paper; top with a wire rack.
2. In the top of a double boiler, whisk together egg whites, corn syrup, sugar, salt, and cream of tartar. Cook over simmering water, stirring constantly, until sugar dissolves and an instant-read thermometer registers 160°F (71°C), about 7 minutes.
3. Carefully transfer mixture to the bowl of a stand mixer. Using the whisk attachment, beat at high speed until doubled in volume and stiff peaks form, 3 to 4 minutes. Beat in vanilla.
4. Spoon marshmallow into a pastry bag fitted with a medium round piping tip. Using even pressure, pipe a "kiss" shape onto each Gingersnap. Let stand until marshmallow is set, about 20 minutes.
5. In a medium microwave-safe bowl, heat chocolate wafers on high in 30-second intervals, stirring between each, until melted and smooth. Dip marshmallow-topped Gingersnaps in melted chocolate, and place on prepared rack. (Melted chocolate can also be spooned onto marshmallow if you prefer.) Let stand until chocolate is set. Store in an airtight container for up to 3 days.

Gingersnaps

Makes about 60 cookies

- 1 cup (227 grams) unsalted butter, softened
- 1⅓ cups (267 grams) granulated sugar
- 1 large egg (50 grams), room temperature
- 1 large egg yolk (19 grams), room temperature
- ½ teaspoon (2 grams) vanilla extract
- ⅓ cup (113 grams) molasses
- 3 cups (375 grams) all-purpose flour, plus more for dusting
- 2½ teaspoons (12.5 grams) baking soda
- 2½ teaspoons (5 grams) ground cinnamon
- 2½ teaspoons (5 grams) ground ginger
- ¾ teaspoon (2.25 grams) kosher salt
- ¼ teaspoon ground black pepper
- ¼ cup (43 grams) diced crystallized ginger

1. In the bowl of stand mixer fitted with the paddle attachment, beat butter and sugar at medium speed until fluffy, 3 to 4 minutes, stopping to scrape sides of bowl. Add egg, egg yolk, and vanilla, beating just until combined. Beat in molasses.
2. In a large bowl, whisk together flour, baking soda, cinnamon, ground ginger, salt, and pepper. With mixer on low speed, gradually add flour mixture to butter mixture, beating just until combined. Add crystallized ginger, beating until combined.
3. On a heavily floured surface, divide dough in half. Shape each half into a 2-inch-diameter log. Wrap tightly in plastic wrap, and freeze until firm, at least 1 hour, or for up to 3 months. If fully frozen, let thaw in refrigerator before slicing.
4. Preheat oven to 325°F (170°C). Line baking sheets with parchment paper.
5. Working with 1 log at a time, cut crosswise into ¼-inch-thick slices. Place on prepared pans.
6. Bake until edges are browned, 10 to 14 minutes. Let cool completely on wire racks. Store in an airtight container for up to 5 days.

Cream Cheese-Stuffed Red Velvet Cookies

Makes about 28 cookies

Moist and chewy red velvet cookies get a dollop of sweetened cream cheese stuffed in the center and a decorative white chocolate drizzle. Each cookie looks like a perfectly wrapped present with a sweet surprise inside.

1½ cups (340 grams) unsalted butter, softened
2¼ cups (450 grams) plus 3½ tablespoons (42 grams) granulated sugar, divided
3 large eggs (150 grams), room temperature
2 tablespoons (30 grams) red liquid food coloring
1½ teaspoons (6 grams) vanilla extract
4½ cups (563 grams) all-purpose flour
½ cup (43 grams) unsweetened cocoa powder, sifted
1½ tablespoons (22.5 grams) baking powder
½ teaspoon kosher salt, divided
8 ounces (226 grams) cream cheese, room temperature
Garnish: melted white chocolate

1. In the bowl of a stand mixer fitted with the paddle attachment, beat butter and 2¼ cups (450 grams) granulated sugar at medium speed until light and fluffy, 3 to 4 minutes, stopping to scrape sides of bowl. Add eggs, one at a time, beating well after each addition. Beat in food coloring and vanilla.
2. In a medium bowl, whisk together flour, cocoa, baking powder, and ¼ teaspoon salt. With mixer on low speed, gradually add flour mixture to butter mixture, beating just until combined and stopping to scrape sides of bowl. Cover and refrigerate until dough no longer sticks to your fingers when pinched, 30 to 45 minutes.
3. In another medium bowl, stir together cream cheese, remaining 3½ tablespoons (42 grams) granulated sugar, and remaining ¼ teaspoon salt. Cover and freeze for 15 minutes.
4. Preheat oven to 350°F (180°C). Line baking sheets with parchment paper.
5. Using a 1½-tablespoon (about 26 grams) spring-loaded scoop, scoop dough, and roll into balls. Press balls into 2½-inch disks. Place 1½ teaspoons (9 grams) cream cheese mixture each in center of half of disks; cover with remaining disks, and crimp edges closed. Gently shape into balls, and place 3 inches apart on prepared pans; gently press into 2¼-inch disks, pressing together any cracks in edges, if necessary. (Refrigerate assembled disks until ready to bake.)
6. Bake, one pan at a time, until edges are dry and centers are slightly wet and puffed, 8 to 10 minutes. Let cool on pan for 5 minutes. Remove from pan, and let cool completely on wire racks. Garnish with melted white chocolate, if desired.

Stuffed Hazelnut-Chocolate Crinkles

Makes about 13 cookies

Chopped hazelnuts scattered throughout the batter add a slight crunch to these soft and tender cookies.

- **1 cup (292 grams) hazelnut chocolate spread, divided**
- **½ cup (113 grams) unsalted butter, cubed and softened**
- **¾ cup (150 grams) granulated sugar**
- **¼ cup (55 grams) firmly packed light brown sugar**
- **1 large egg (50 grams)**
- **1 teaspoon (4 grams) vanilla extract**
- **2 cups (250 grams) all-purpose flour**
- **1½ teaspoons (7.5 grams) baking powder**
- **½ teaspoon (1.5 grams) kosher salt**
- **⅓ cup (38 grams) finely chopped hazelnuts**

Garnish: confectioners' sugar

1. Line baking sheets with parchment paper.
2. In the bowl of a stand mixer fitted with the paddle attachment, beat ½ cup (146 grams) hazelnut chocolate spread and butter at medium speed until smooth and combined. Add granulated sugar and brown sugar; beat at medium-high speed until light and fluffy, 2 to 3 minutes, stopping to scrape sides of bowl. Beat in egg and vanilla until combined, stopping to scrape sides of bowl.
3. In a medium bowl, whisk together flour, baking powder, and salt. Add flour mixture to butter mixture, and beat at low speed just until combined. Fold in hazelnuts. Using a 1½-tablespoon (about 30 grams) spring-loaded scoop, scoop dough, and roll into balls. Flatten dough balls into 2½-inch rounds. Spoon 1 heaping teaspoon (about 6 grams) hazelnut chocolate spread into center of half of dough rounds (you'll have leftover spread). Cover with remaining dough rounds, and gently crimp edges to seal. Place 2½ inches apart on prepared pans. Refrigerate for at least 30 minutes.
4. Preheat oven to 350°F (180°C).
5. Gently shape dough to be about 2½ inches in diameter, smoothing edges.
6. Bake until lightly puffed, tops look dry, and edges are set, 13 to 16 minutes. Let cool completely on pans on wire racks. Garnish with confectioners' sugar, if desired. Store in an airtight container for up to 3 days.

Cream Cheese-Filled Chocolate Chip Cookies

Makes 24 cookies

Because I believe you can never have too much of a good thing, I decided to add cream cheese to both chocolate chip cookie dough and as a filling for the cookies. It turns an already great cookie into an extravagance—emphasis on the "extra."

- ½ cup (113 grams) unsalted butter, softened
- 10 ounces (284 grams) cream cheese, softened and divided
- ⅔ cup (147 grams) firmly packed dark brown sugar
- ⅓ cup (67 grams) plus 3½ tablespoons (42 grams) granulated sugar, divided
- 1 large egg (50 grams), room temperature
- 1 tablespoon (13 grams) vanilla extract
- 2 cups (250 grams) all-purpose flour
- 1½ teaspoons (4.5 grams) cornstarch
- 1 teaspoon (5 grams) baking soda
- 1 teaspoon (2.25 grams) kosher salt, divided
- 4.5 ounces (128 grams) milk chocolate, chopped (about ¾ cup)
- 3 ounces (85 grams) semisweet chocolate, chopped (about ½ cup)

Pro Tip

Cookie dough and cream cheese filling can be made a day ahead, covered, and refrigerated separately overnight. Let each stand at room temperature until softened, about 30 minutes. Shape and bake as directed.

1. In the bowl of a stand mixer fitted with the paddle attachment, beat butter at medium speed until smooth and creamy, about 1 minute. Add 2 ounces (57 grams) cream cheese; beat until smooth and well combined, about 30 seconds, stopping to scrape paddle and bottom and sides of bowl. Add brown sugar and ⅓ cup (67 grams) granulated sugar; beat until fluffy, about 2 minutes, stopping to scrape paddle and bottom and sides of bowl. Add egg and vanilla; beat until combined.

2. In a large bowl, whisk together flour, cornstarch, baking soda, and ¾ teaspoon (2.25 grams) salt. Add flour mixture to butter mixture; beat at low speed just until combined. Fold in all chocolate. Cover and refrigerate for 30 minutes.

3. Preheat oven to 350°F (180°C). Line rimmed baking sheets with parchment paper.

4. In a medium bowl, stir together remaining 8 ounces (227 grams) cream cheese, remaining 3½ tablespoons (42 grams) granulated sugar, and remaining ¼ teaspoon salt. Cover and freeze for 15 minutes.

5. Divide dough into 48 portions (about 1 tablespoon or 18 grams each); shape each portion into a ball, and flatten into 1½- to 2-inch disks. Spoon about 1½ teaspoons (9 grams) cream cheese mixture in center of 1 dough disk, and cover with a second disk. Crimp edges to seal, and gently shape into a ball. Repeat with remaining dough disks and remaining cream cheese mixture. Place dough balls 1½ to 2 inches apart on prepared pans. Gently flatten balls to ¾-inch thickness, crimping any cracks to seal.

6. Bake until edges are set and lightly browned, 8 to 10 minutes. Let cool on pans for 2 minutes. Remove from pans, and let cool completely on wire racks. Store in an airtight container for up to 3 days.

Fresh and Fruity

Produce-filled delights burst with vibrant flavors, from tropical cookie bars to citrusy madeleines, infusing freshness into every sweet bite

Banana Bread Cookies

Makes 24 cookies

I've never met a banana bread I didn't like, so I thought, why not turn it into a soft, cake-like cookie? Sweet success!

- ⅔ cup (150 grams) unsalted butter, softened
- 1⅓ cups (267 grams) granulated sugar
- 1 cup (220 grams) firmly packed light brown sugar
- 1 large egg (50 grams)
- ½ cup (114 grams) mashed ripe banana
- 1 tablespoon (13 grams) plus ⅛ teaspoon vanilla extract, divided
- 4 cups (500 grams) all-purpose flour
- 4 teaspoons (20 grams) baking powder
- 1½ teaspoons (4.5 grams) kosher salt
- 1 cup (240 grams) sour cream
- 1 cup (113 grams) chopped pecans
- ¾ cup (150 grams) chopped banana
- Pecan Streusel (recipe follows)
- 1½ cups (180 grams) confectioners' sugar
- 2½ tablespoons (37.5 grams) whole milk

1. Preheat oven to 375°F (190°C). Line baking sheets with parchment paper.

2. In the bowl of a stand mixer fitted with the paddle attachment, beat butter and sugars at medium speed until fluffy, 3 to 4 minutes, stopping to scrape paddle and bottom and sides of bowl. Add egg, beating well. Beat in mashed banana and 1 tablespoon (13 grams) vanilla.

3. In a medium bowl, whisk together flour, baking powder, and salt. With mixer on low speed, gradually add flour mixture to butter mixture in two additions alternately with sour cream, beginning and ending with flour mixture, beating just until combined after each addition. Stir in pecans and chopped banana.

4. Using a ¼-cup spring-loaded scoop, scoop batter, and place at least 2 inches apart on prepared pans. Sprinkle with half of Pecan Streusel.

5. Bake for 6 minutes. Sprinkle with remaining Pecan Streusel, filling any empty spaces on top. Bake until a wooden pick inserted in center comes out clean, 6 to 8 minutes more. Let cool on pans for 5 minutes. Remove from pans, and let cool completely on wire racks.

6. In a small bowl, whisk together confectioners' sugar, milk, and remaining ⅛ teaspoon vanilla until smooth. Drizzle onto cooled cookies. Refrigerate in an airtight container for up to 3 days.

Pecan Streusel

Makes about 2½ cups

- ⅔ cup (83 grams) all-purpose flour
- 6 tablespoons (72 grams) granulated sugar
- ¼ cup (55 grams) firmly packed light brown sugar
- ½ teaspoon (1.5 grams) kosher salt
- ½ teaspoon (1 gram) ground cinnamon
- 6 tablespoons (84 grams) cold unsalted butter, cubed
- 1 cup (113 grams) chopped pecans

1. In a medium bowl, stir together flour, sugars, salt, and cinnamon. Using your fingers, cut in cold butter until mixture is crumbly and desired consistency is reached. Stir in pecans. Refrigerate until ready to use.

Pro Tip

Bananas are excellent produce to stock in the freezer. Keep the bananas in their peel (this protects them from freezer burn and odors), and store in a resealable plastic freezer bag. Once you're ready to bake, let the bananas thaw before peeling. The bananas should come out as purée—freezing breaks down their cell walls and softens them.

Hummingbird Cookie Bars

Makes 24 bars

These party-worthy bars are creamy, crumbly, and crispy all at once. For the best flavor and texture, I suggest refrigerating overnight, but you can cut that time down to at least 1 hour before serving.

- **12 ounces (340 grams) cream cheese, softened**
- **¼ cup (50 grams) granulated sugar**
- **2 large eggs (100 grams)**
- **2 teaspoons (8 grams) vanilla extract**
- **½ cup (114 grams) mashed ripe banana**
- Spiced Cookie Crust (recipe follows)
- **2 cups (400 grams) diced fresh pineapple**
- **1⅓ cups (80 grams) sweetened flaked coconut**
- **1 cup (113 grams) chopped pecans**
- **½ cup (44 grams) broken banana chips**
- **¼ cup (57 grams) unsalted butter, melted**

1. Preheat oven to 350°F (180°C).
2. In the bowl of a stand mixer fitted with the paddle attachment, beat cream cheese and sugar at medium speed until creamy, 3 to 4 minutes, stopping to scrape paddle and bottom and sides of bowl. Add eggs and vanilla, beating until well combined. Fold in mashed banana. Spread cream cheese mixture onto prepared Spiced Cookie Crust. Sprinkle pineapple on top.
3. In a medium bowl, stir together coconut, pecans, banana chips, and melted butter until well combined. Sprinkle onto pineapple.
4. Bake until filling is set, 35 to 40 minutes, covering with foil to prevent excess browning, if necessary. Let cool completely in pan on a wire rack. Refrigerate overnight. Using excess parchment as handles, remove from pan, and cut into bars. Refrigerate in an airtight container for up to 3 days.

Spiced Cookie Crust

Makes 1 (13x9-inch) crust

- **2 cups (250 grams) all-purpose flour**
- **½ cup (100 grams) granulated sugar**
- **¾ teaspoon (1.5 grams) ground cinnamon**
- **½ teaspoon (1.5 grams) kosher salt**
- **¼ teaspoon ground nutmeg**
- **¾ cup (170 grams) unsalted butter, cubed and softened**

1. Preheat oven to 350°F (180°C). Spray a 13x9-inch baking dish with cooking spray. Line pan with parchment paper, letting excess extend over sides of pan.
2. In a medium bowl, whisk together flour, sugar, cinnamon, salt, and nutmeg. Using a pastry blender, cut in butter until mixture is crumbly. Firmly press mixture into bottom of prepared pan.
3. Bake until lightly browned, about 40 minutes. Let cool completely.

Pro Tip

Overripe bananas on the verge of spoiling are best for baking. They bring deep flavor and moisture to your baked goods.

Apricot Macaroons

Makes about 20 cookies

These fruit-studded mounds are likely the easiest and most forgiving of all cookies. Crunchy on the outside and meltingly chewy within, they take only moments to whip up and keep well. In addition to a cheerful pop of color, dried apricots have an inherent tartness, which balances the cookies' sweetness beautifully.

- **4 large egg whites (120 grams), room temperature**
- **½ cup (100 grams) granulated sugar**
- **½ teaspoon (2 grams) vanilla extract**
- **1 (14-ounce) package (396 grams) sweetened flaked coconut**
- **½ cup (90 grams) chopped dried apricots**
- **½ teaspoon (1.5 grams) kosher salt**

1. Preheat oven to 300°F (150°C). Line baking sheets with parchment paper.

2. In the bowl of a stand mixer fitted with the paddle attachment, beat egg whites at medium speed until foamy, 4 to 5 minutes. Add sugar and vanilla, beating until combined. Fold in coconut, apricots, and salt. Using a 1½-tablespoon (about 30 grams) spring-loaded scoop, scoop dough, and place 2 inches apart on prepared pans.

3. Bake until edges are lightly browned, 22 to 25 minutes. Let cool on pans for 5 minutes. Using a rubber spatula, remove from pans, and let cool completely on wire racks. Refrigerate in an airtight container for up to 3 days.

Fig Bars

Makes about 40 bars

Fig Newtons have seen the inside of lunch boxes and snack bags since they were first mass-produced more than 130 years ago. My homemade version features a rich, buttery dough surrounding a thick filling of Mission figs, which are sweeter and softer than other fig varieties, plus fresh orange zest and juice for a bright citrus accent.

Dough:

- ⅔ cup (150 grams) unsalted butter, softened
- ½ cup (110 grams) firmly packed light brown sugar
- 1 teaspoon (1 gram) orange zest
- 1 large egg (50 grams), room temperature
- ½ teaspoon (2 grams) vanilla extract
- 2⅓ cups (292 grams) all-purpose flour, plus more for dusting
- ½ teaspoon (2.5 grams) baking soda
- ¼ teaspoon kosher salt
- ¼ teaspoon ground cinnamon
- 2 tablespoons (30 grams) fresh orange juice

Filling:

- 10 ounces (283 grams) dried black Mission figs, stemmed and halved
- ¾ cup (180 grams) water
- ¼ cup (60 grams) fresh orange juice
- ¼ cup (85 grams) honey
- ¼ teaspoon ground cinnamon

1. For dough: In the bowl of a stand mixer fitted with the paddle attachment, beat butter, brown sugar, and orange zest at medium speed until pale and creamy, 2 to 3 minutes, stopping to scrape sides of bowl. Beat in egg and vanilla, stopping to scrape sides of bowl.

2. In a medium bowl, whisk together flour, baking soda, salt, and cinnamon. With mixer on low speed, gradually add flour mixture to butter mixture alternately with orange juice, beating until just combined after each addition. Turn out dough onto a sheet of plastic wrap, and shape dough into a rectangle. Wrap in plastic wrap, and refrigerate until firm, at least 1 hour.

3. For filling: In a small saucepan, bring figs, ¾ cup (180 grams) water, and orange juice to a boil over medium heat. Reduce heat, and simmer, stirring occasionally, until almost all liquid has evaporated and figs have plumped, 7 to 10 minutes.

4. In the work bowl of a food processor, pulse fig mixture, honey, and cinnamon until a thick paste forms. Let cool completely.

5. Preheat oven to 350°F (180°C). Line 2 baking sheets with parchment paper.

6. On a lightly floured surface, roll dough into a 13½-inch square. Trim ⅛ inch off each side of dough. Cut dough into 4 (13x3¼-inch) strips.

7. Spoon cooled filling into a pastry bag, and cut a ½-inch opening in tip. Pipe a 1-inch-wide strip of filling down center of each dough strip. Using a pastry brush, brush off excess flour. Working with 1 strip at a time, fold sides of dough strip over filling, gently pressing seams to seal. (When folding, make sure there are no gaps between dough and filling.) Place dough logs, seam side down, on prepared pans.

8. Bake until edges are golden brown, 18 to 20 minutes. Using a bench scraper or sharp knife, immediately cut each log crosswise into 1½-inch-wide pieces; leave cookies on pans and touching each other. Let cool for 15 minutes. Remove from pans, and let cool completely on wire racks. Store in an airtight container for up to 5 days.

Chewy Oatmeal-Raisin Cookies

Makes 18 cookies

These grown-up–portioned treats bake up soft from edge to edge and stay that way for several days thanks to moisture-attracting brown sugar and soft raisins in the dough. Use a mix of dark and golden raisins, all golden raisins, or add a handful of chopped nuts if you like.

- ½ cup (113 grams) unsalted butter, softened
- ¾ cup (165 grams) firmly packed light brown sugar
- ⅓ cup (67 grams) granulated sugar
- 2 large eggs (100 grams), room temperature
- 1 teaspoon (4 grams) vanilla extract
- 2 cups (180 grams) old-fashioned oats
- 1 cup (125 grams) all-purpose flour
- 1 teaspoon (2 grams) ground cinnamon
- ¾ teaspoon (3.75 grams) baking soda
- ½ teaspoon (1.5 grams) kosher salt
- ¼ teaspoon (1.25 grams) baking powder
- 1 cup (128 grams) raisins

1. Line rimmed baking sheets with parchment paper.

2. In the bowl of a stand mixer fitted with the paddle attachment, beat butter and sugars at medium speed until light and fluffy, 2 to 3 minutes, stopping to scrape sides of bowl. Add eggs, one at a time, beating well after each addition and stopping to scrape sides of bowl. Beat in vanilla.

3. In a medium bowl, whisk together oats, flour, cinnamon, baking soda, salt, and baking powder. With mixer on low speed, gradually add oats mixture to butter mixture, beating just until combined. Stir in raisins. Using a 3-tablespoon (about 52 grams) spring-loaded scoop, scoop dough, and place about 2 inches apart on prepared pans. Refrigerate until firm, about 30 minutes.

4. Preheat oven to 325°F (170°C).

5. Bake until edges are just set, about 18 minutes. (Centers will still seem a little soft.) Let cool on pans for 5 minutes. Remove from pans, and let cool completely on wire racks. Store in an airtight container for up to 3 days.

Apple-Honey Cookies

Makes about 15 cookies

A thin slice of apple tops these soft cookies spiced with the triple threat of cinnamon, ginger, and cloves. Apples and honey are traditionally found in Jewish baking and are especially enjoyed together on Rosh Hashanah as a symbol of a sweet new year ahead.

¾ cup (170 grams) unsalted butter, softened
1 cup (200 grams) granulated sugar
¼ cup (85 grams) honey
1 large egg (50 grams), room temperature
1 large egg yolk (19 grams), room temperature
1 teaspoon (4 grams) vanilla extract
2½ cups (313 grams) all-purpose flour
2 teaspoons (4 grams) ground cinnamon
½ teaspoon (2.5 grams) baking powder
½ teaspoon (2.5 grams) baking soda
½ teaspoon (1.5 grams) kosher salt
½ teaspoon (1 gram) ground ginger
⅛ teaspoon ground cloves
1 to 2 small Gala apples (160 to 320 grams), cut crosswise into ⅛-inch-thick slices

1. In the bowl of a stand mixer fitted with the paddle attachment, beat butter, sugar, and honey at medium speed until light and fluffy, 2 to 3 minutes, stopping to scrape bottom and sides of bowl. Beat in egg, egg yolk, and vanilla, stopping to scrape bottom and sides of bowl.
2. In a medium bowl, whisk together flour, cinnamon, baking powder, baking soda, salt, ginger, and cloves. With mixer on low speed, gradually add flour mixture to butter mixture, beating until just combined and no dry streaks remain. Cover bowl, and refrigerate for 1 hour.
3. Preheat oven to 375°F (190°C). Line baking sheets with parchment paper.
4. Using a 3-tablespoon (about 50 grams) spring-loaded scoop, scoop dough, and roll into balls. Place 2 inches apart on prepared pans. Top each with 1 apple slice, and gently flatten into a ½-inch-thick circle (including height of apple slice).
5. Bake until edges of cookies are golden brown and set, 10 to 15 minutes. Let cool on pans for 10 minutes. Remove from pans, and let cool completely on wire racks. Store in an airtight container for up to 3 days.

Lemon-Poppy Seed Hamantaschen

Makes 18 cookies

Poppy seeds are the traditional filling of these cookies, which are associated with the Jewish holiday Purim. The name refers to the villain of the Purim story, Haman.

Filling:

- **⅓ cup (47 grams) poppy seeds**
- **4 tablespoons (48 grams) granulated sugar, divided**
- **¼ teaspoon kosher salt**
- **⅓ cup (80 grams) whole milk**
- **2 tablespoons (28 grams) unsalted butter**
- **1 large egg yolk (19 grams)**
- **1 teaspoon (1 gram) lemon zest**

Dough:

- **¾ cup (170 grams) unsalted butter, softened**
- **1¼ cups (150 grams) confectioners' sugar**
- **1 tablespoon (3 grams) lemon zest**
- **1 large egg (50 grams), room temperature**
- **1 teaspoon (4 grams) vanilla extract**
- **2¾ cups (344 grams) all-purpose flour, plus more for dusting**
- **½ teaspoon (1.5 grams) kosher salt**

Pro Tip

A spice grinder (or, alternatively, a mortar and pestle) works best for grinding the poppy seeds into a paste for the filling; the seeds are too small to adequately make contact with the blade of a food processor or mixer.

1. For filling: In a spice grinder, process poppy seeds, 2 tablespoons (24 grams) granulated sugar, and salt until finely ground, 3 to 4 minutes.
2. In a small saucepan, heat milk and butter over medium heat until bubbles form around sides of pan. (Do not boil.)
3. In a medium heatproof bowl, whisk together egg yolk, lemon zest, and remaining 2 tablespoons (24 grams) granulated sugar. Slowly add hot milk mixture, whisking constantly. Pour egg yolk mixture into saucepan; cook over medium-low heat, whisking frequently, until thickened, 1 to 2 minutes. Strain mixture through a fine-mesh sieve into another medium heatproof bowl. Stir in poppy seed mixture. Cover with plastic wrap, pressing wrap directly onto surface of filling to prevent a skin from forming. Refrigerate until chilled, at least 1 hour.
4. For dough: In the bowl of a stand mixer fitted with the paddle attachment, beat butter, confectioners' sugar, and lemon zest at medium speed until creamy, 3 to 4 minutes, stopping to scrape sides of bowl. Beat in egg and vanilla.
5. In a medium bowl, whisk together flour and salt. With mixer on low speed, gradually add flour mixture to butter mixture, beating until a smooth dough forms. Turn out dough, and press into a rectangle (about 1 inch thick). Wrap in plastic wrap, and refrigerate until firm, about 30 minutes.
6. Line 2 rimmed baking sheets with parchment paper.
7. On a lightly floured surface, roll dough to ¼-inch thickness. (If the dough is too stiff, let stand at room temperature for 15 minutes.) Using a 3¼-inch round cutter, cut dough, rerolling scraps as necessary. Spoon 2 teaspoons (10 grams) filling into center of each dough circle. Fold dough in from three sides, overlapping at corners, and pinch edges together to seal, leaving a small opening over filling. Place 2 inches apart on prepared pans. Refrigerate for 1 hour.
8. Preheat oven to 350°F (180°C).
9. Re-pinch corners of hamantaschen to ensure they're well sealed.
10. Bake until bottoms and corners are golden brown, 20 to 25 minutes, rotating pans halfway through baking. Let cool completely on pans on wire racks. Store in an airtight container for up to 3 days.

Lime-Mint Crinkles

Makes 36 cookies

Finely chopped fresh mint and heaps of lime zest come together in one irresistible cookie that's reminiscent of an ice-cold mojito. Keep the cookies au naturel or add a touch of green gel food coloring to intensify the confectioners' sugar crackle.

- **2 cups (250 grams) all-purpose flour**
- **¾ teaspoon (2.25 grams) kosher salt**
- **½ teaspoon (2.5 grams) baking soda**
- **1⅓ cups (267 grams) granulated sugar, divided**
- **3 tablespoons (8 grams) lightly packed finely chopped fresh mint**
- **2 tablespoons (8 grams) packed lime zest (about 5 large limes)**
- **½ cup (113 grams) unsalted butter, melted and cooled for 5 minutes**
- **1 large egg (50 grams), room temperature**
- **1 large egg yolk (19 grams), room temperature**
- **2 tablespoons (30 grams) fresh lime juice**
- **Green gel food coloring (optional)**
- **½ cup (60 grams) confectioners' sugar, sifted**

NOTE: *If cookie dough begins to get too soft, refrigerate it until firm, 10 to 15 minutes.*

1. In a medium bowl, whisk together flour, salt, and baking soda.
2. In a large bowl, whisk together 1 cup (200 grams) granulated sugar, mint, and lime zest until well combined and fragrant. Whisk in melted butter, egg, and egg yolk. Whisk in lime juice.
3. Add flour mixture to sugar mixture in two additions, folding until well combined after each addition. Fold in food coloring (if using) until desired color is reached. Cover and refrigerate for at least 2 hours.
4. Preheat oven to 350°F (180°C). Line rimmed baking sheets with parchment paper.
5. In a small bowl, place confectioners' sugar. In another small bowl, place remaining ⅓ cup (67 grams) granulated sugar.
6. Divide dough into 36 portions (about 18 grams each), and shape each portion into a ball. Roll balls in granulated sugar; roll in confectioners' sugar. Place 2 inches apart on prepared pans.
7. Bake until edges and tops are just set and cracks have formed, 8 to 10 minutes. Let cool completely on pans on wire racks. Store in an airtight container for up to 3 days.

Lemon-Raspberry Marble Cookies

Makes about 32 cookies

Marble cookies are deceptively easy to make and create a stunning presentation. Simply take equal-size portions of alternating dough flavors, roll together, and bake!

- 1 cup (227 grams) unsalted butter, softened
- 1¾ cups (350 grams) granulated sugar, divided
- 1 tablespoon (3 grams) lemon zest (about 3 medium lemons)
- 1 large egg (50 grams), room temperature
- 2 tablespoons (30 grams) fresh lemon juice
- 1 teaspoon (4 grams) vanilla extract
- 2¾ cups (344 grams) all-purpose flour
- 1¼ teaspoons (3.75 grams) kosher salt
- 1 teaspoon (5 grams) baking soda
- ½ teaspoon (2.5 grams) baking powder
- ¾ cup (30 grams) sifted finely crushed freeze-dried raspberries (see Note)
- Pink gel food coloring

NOTE: *Crush and sift your freeze-dried fruit before measuring; removing the seeds intensifies the color of the dough and ensures the cookie is pleasant to eat.*

1. Preheat oven to 350°F (180°C). Line rimmed baking sheets with parchment paper.

2. In the bowl of a stand mixer fitted with the paddle attachment, beat butter, 1½ cups (300 grams) sugar, and lemon zest at medium speed until fluffy, 2 to 3 minutes, stopping to scrape paddle and bottom and sides of bowl. Beat in egg. Beat in lemon juice and vanilla.

3. In a medium bowl, whisk together flour, salt, baking soda, and baking powder. Add flour mixture to butter mixture; beat at medium-low speed just until combined, stopping to scrape bottom and sides of bowl.

4. Transfer half of dough (about 1½ cups or about 470 grams) to a medium bowl. Add raspberries and desired amount of food coloring to remaining dough; beat at medium-low speed until combined, kneading together by hand toward end, if necessary.

5. In a small bowl, place remaining ½ cup (50 grams) sugar.

6. Scoop lemon dough by teaspoonfuls (about 7 grams each); scoop raspberry dough by teaspoonfuls (about 7 grams each). Layer and press together 2 lemon dough scoops and 2 raspberry dough scoops in an alternating fashion; roll into a ball, pinching together any seams, and roll in sugar. Place at least 2 inches apart on prepared pans. Repeat procedure with remaining dough. Refrigerate for 30 minutes.

7. Bake, one pan at a time, until edges and tops look just set and some small cracks are starting to form but centers seem puffed and slightly underdone, 8 to 10 minutes, rotating pan halfway through baking. Let cool on pan for 5 minutes. Remove from pan, and let cool completely on wire racks. Store in an airtight container for up to 3 days.

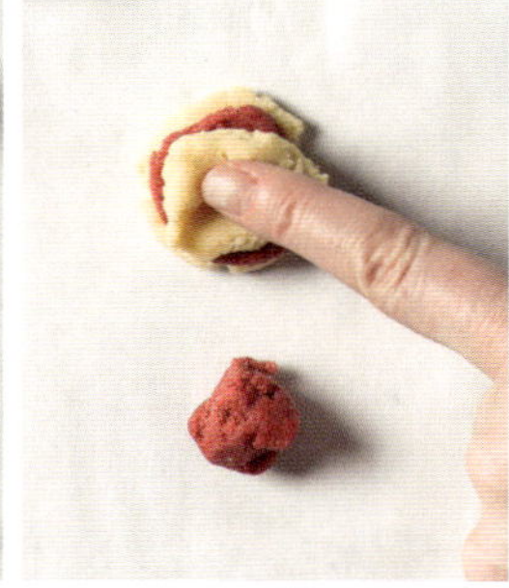

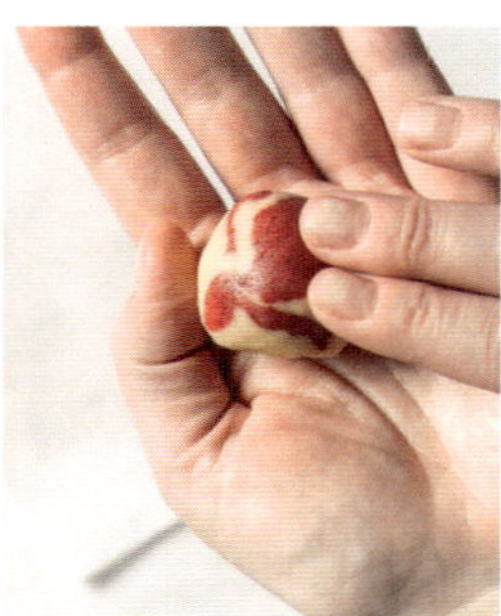

Tangerine Madeleines

Makes 24 madeleines

Fresh citrus zest is an elegantly simple enhancement to this classic French cookie.

- **1¾ cups (219 grams) all-purpose flour**
- **1½ teaspoons (7.5 grams) baking powder**
- **¼ teaspoon kosher salt**
- **1 cup (200 grams) granulated sugar**
- **5 large eggs (250 grams)**
- **2 tablespoons (12 grams) tangerine zest**
- **1 cup (227 grams) unsalted butter, melted**
- **¼ teaspoon (1 gram) vanilla extract**
- **Confectioners' sugar, for dusting**

1. In a medium bowl, whisk together flour, baking powder, and salt.

2. In a large bowl, whisk together granulated sugar, eggs, and tangerine zest. Add flour mixture, stirring just until combined. Add melted butter and vanilla in a slow, steady stream, whisking constantly until batter becomes cohesive. Cover and refrigerate until completely cooled, at least 2 hours.

3. Preheat oven to 325°F (170°C). Spray 2 madeleine pans with cooking spray.

4. Spoon batter by teaspoonfuls into prepared pans. (Do not spread batter to fill wells of pan.)

5. Bake until golden brown, 10 to 15 minutes. Let cool in pans for 5 minutes. Remove from pans, dust with confectioners' sugar, and serve immediately. Store in an airtight container for up to 3 days.

Browned Butter Apricot Blondies

Makes 9 blondies

The blondie—that golden, caramelized bar that verges on butterscotch bliss—was begging for a swirl of something tangy-sweet. Enter a homemade apricot jam. I added a hefty dose of nutty browned butter for good measure and finished them with a light sprinkle of sea salt.

- **½ cup (113 grams) unsalted butter**
- **1¼ cups (156 grams) all-purpose flour**
- **1 teaspoon (5 grams) baking powder**
- **½ teaspoon (1.5 grams) kosher salt**
- **1 teaspoon (4 grams) vanilla extract**
- **1 cup (220 grams) firmly packed light brown sugar**
- **2 large eggs (100 grams)**
- **¼ cup (80 grams) Apricot Jam (recipe follows)**
- **Garnish: flaked sea salt**

1. Preheat oven to 350°F (180°C). Spray a 9-inch square baking dish with baking spray with flour.

2. In a medium saucepan, melt butter over medium heat. Cook, stirring frequently, until butter turns a medium-brown color and has a nutty aroma, about 10 minutes. Remove from heat.

3. In a large bowl, whisk together flour, baking powder, and kosher salt. Whisk in melted browned butter and vanilla. (Mixture will be thick.)

4. In the bowl of a stand mixer fitted with the whisk attachment, beat brown sugar and eggs at high speed until tripled in size, 4 to 5 minutes. Add one-third of sugar mixture to flour mixture, stirring just until combined. Fold in remaining sugar mixture in two additions until well combined. Pour into prepared pan. Spoon Apricot Jam, 1 to 2 teaspoons (7 to 14 grams) at a time, onto batter.

5. Bake until a wooden pick inserted in center comes out clean, 20 to 30 minutes. Garnish with sea salt, if desired. Let cool completely in pan on a wire rack. Store in an airtight container for up to 4 days.

Apricot Jam

Makes about 2 cups

- **3 cups (480 grams) chopped fresh apricots**
- **1½ cups (300 grams) granulated sugar**
- **1 teaspoon (1 gram) lemon zest**
- **1 tablespoon (15 grams) fresh lemon juice**
- **½ teaspoon (1.5 grams) kosher salt**
- **½ teaspoon (1 gram) ground black pepper**

1. In a medium saucepan, bring all ingredients to a boil over medium-high heat. Cook, stirring frequently, for 5 minutes. Reduce heat to medium; cook, stirring frequently, until mixture thickens, 20 to 45 minutes. Remove from heat, and let cool completely. Refrigerate in an airtight container for up to 2 weeks.

Orange-Chocolate Brownie Cookies

Makes about 9 cookies

Acidity from the candied orange peel perfectly cuts through the decadence of the chocolate in this delectably fudgy, faultlessly chewy cookie.

- **7 ounces (198 grams) bittersweet chocolate baking bars, chopped and divided**
- **3 tablespoons (42 grams) unsalted butter, softened**
- **¼ cup (50 grams) granulated sugar**
- **¼ cup (55 grams) firmly packed light brown sugar**
- **1 teaspoon (1 gram) instant espresso powder**
- **1 teaspoon (4 grams) vanilla extract**
- **½ teaspoon (1 gram) packed orange zest**
- **¼ teaspoon kosher salt**
- **1 large egg (50 grams), room temperature**
- **½ cup (63 grams) all-purpose flour**
- **2 tablespoons (10 grams) Dutch process cocoa powder**
- **½ teaspoon (2.5 grams) baking powder**
- **⅓ cup (59 grams) plus 1½ tablespoons (17 grams) lightly packed minced candied orange peel, divided**

1. In the top of a double boiler, heat 4 ounces (113 grams) chocolate and butter over simmering water, stirring occasionally, until melted and smooth. Remove from heat; whisk in sugars, espresso powder, vanilla, orange zest, and salt until well combined. Let cool for 5 minutes. Whisk in egg.

2. In a medium bowl, whisk together flour, cocoa, and baking powder. Add flour mixture to chocolate mixture, stirring until just a few bits of flour remain. Fold in ⅓ cup (59 grams) candied orange peel and 2 ounces (57 grams) chocolate. Cover and refrigerate for 30 minutes.

3. Preheat oven to 350°F (180°C). Line baking sheets with parchment paper.

4. Using a 3-tablespoon (about 53 grams) spring-loaded scoop, scoop dough, and roll into balls. Place 2 inches apart on prepared pans; flatten each dough ball into a 2¼-inch disk (about ½ inch thick), pressing together any cracks in edges if necessary. Gently press remaining 1 ounce (28 grams) chocolate and remaining 1½ tablespoons (17 grams) candied peel into tops of dough disks.

5. Bake until tops are lightly cracked, edges are set, and centers look slightly underdone, about 10 minutes. Let cool on pans for 5 minutes. Carefully remove from pans, and let cool completely on wire racks. Store in an airtight container for up to 3 days.

Pro Tip

A 3½- to 4-inch round cutter can be used to form still-warm cookies into a more circular shape, if desired. Place cutter around 1 cookie; gently move cutter in a circular clockwise motion while making contact with edges of cookie until desired shape is reached.

Cherry Crème Fraîche Cookies

Makes about 30 cookies

For the holidays, I adore these cookies, which meld together a few of my favorite things: tart dried cherries, crunchy pearl sugar, tangy crème fraîche, and kirsch, a heavenly brandy made from morello cherries.

- **1 cup (142 grams) dried cherries, diced**
- **½ cup (120 grams) kirsch**
- **⅓ cup (76 grams) unsalted butter, softened**
- **¾ cup (150 grams) granulated sugar**
- **1 large egg (50 grams)**
- **2 large egg yolks (37 grams)**
- **½ cup (120 grams) crème fraîche**
- **2½ cups (313 grams) all-purpose flour**
- **½ teaspoon (2.5 grams) baking powder**
- **¼ teaspoon (1.25 grams) baking soda**
- **¼ teaspoon kosher salt**
- **1 cup (200 grams) Swedish pearl sugar**

1. In a small saucepan, bring dried cherries and kirsch to a boil over medium-high heat. Reduce heat to low; cook, stirring occasionally, until almost all liquid has evaporated, 8 to 10 minutes. Remove from heat, and let cool completely.

2. In the bowl of a stand mixer fitted with the paddle attachment, beat butter and granulated sugar at medium speed until light and fluffy, about 2 minutes, stopping to scrape bottom and sides of bowl. Add egg and egg yolks, one at a time, beating until combined after each addition. Add crème fraîche, beating until combined and stopping to scrape sides of bowl.

3. In a medium bowl, whisk together flour, baking powder, baking soda, and salt. With mixer on low speed, gradually add flour mixture to butter mixture, beating until combined. Gently stir in cooled cherry mixture. (Dough will be sticky.) Cover and refrigerate for 30 minutes.

4. Preheat oven to 350°F (180°C). Line baking sheets with parchment paper.

5. In a small bowl, place pearl sugar.

6. Using a 1½-tablespoon (about 30 grams) spring-loaded scoop, scoop dough, and roll into balls. (If dough is too sticky, dampen your hands with water to roll into balls.) Roll balls in pearl sugar, and place 2 inches apart on prepared pans. Flatten slightly with the palm of your hand.

7. Bake, one pan at a time, until cookies are set but not browned, 10 to 12 minutes. Let cool on pans for 5 minutes. Remove from pans, and let cool completely on wire racks. Store in an airtight container for up to 3 days.

Brown Sugar and Spice

This collection marries aromatic cinnamon, ginger, cloves, and more with the molasses-rich sweetness of brown sugar, evoking cozy comfort with every bite

Gingerbread Cookies

Makes 45 cookies

This divine recipe captures everything I adore about baking in the fall: the warmth of robust spices; the deep, rich flavor of molasses; and a surprise ingredient that adds a delicate citrusy note, beautifully complementing this nostalgic cookie. Evaporated milk adds richness and moisture to the dough, which creates a softer, more tender cookie.

- **1½ cups (300 grams) granulated sugar, divided**
- **2 teaspoons (4 grams) ground ginger**
- **1½ teaspoons (7.5 grams) baking soda**
- **1 teaspoon (3 grams) kosher salt**
- **1 teaspoon (2 grams) ground nutmeg**
- **1 teaspoon (2 grams) ground cinnamon**
- **1 cup (227 grams) unsalted butter, melted**
- **1 cup (336 grams) unsulphured molasses**
- **½ cup (120 grams) evaporated milk**
- **¾ teaspoon (3 grams) vanilla extract**
- **¾ teaspoon (3 grams) lemon extract**
- **4½ cups (563 grams) all-purpose flour**

1. In the bowl of a stand mixer, whisk together 1 cup (200 grams) sugar, ginger, baking soda, salt, nutmeg, and cinnamon by hand until well combined. Add melted butter, molasses, evaporated milk, and extracts; using the paddle attachment, beat at medium-low speed until well combined, stopping to scrape paddle and bottom and sides of bowl. With mixer on low speed, add flour, about 1 cup (125 grams) at a time, beating just until combined after each addition and stopping to scrape bottom and sides of bowl. Cover and refrigerate for at least 1 hour or up to overnight.
2. Preheat oven to 350°F (180°C). Line baking sheets with parchment paper.
3. In a shallow bowl, place remaining ½ cup (100 grams) sugar.
4. Using a 1½-tablespoon (about 32 grams) spring-loaded scoop, scoop dough, and roll into balls. Dredge in sugar to coat, and place 2 inches apart on prepared pans.
5. Bake, one pan at a time, until edges are set and tops are puffed and look dry, 10 to 12 minutes. Let cool on pans for 10 minutes. Remove from pans, and let cool completely on wire racks. Store in an airtight container for up to 5 days.

Chewy Brown Sugar Cookies

Makes 40 cookies

These crispy-edged, chewy-centered cookies get a double dose of rich caramel flavor from browned butter and brown sugar. It's a good thing this recipe creates a lot of cookies because they'll be gone in a flash.

1¼ cups plus 2 tablespoons (312 grams) unsalted butter
2 cups (440 grams) firmly packed light brown sugar
1 large egg (50 grams), room temperature
2 teaspoons (8 grams) vanilla extract
2½ cups (313 grams) all-purpose flour
1 tablespoon (8 grams) cornstarch
1 teaspoon (3 grams) kosher salt
½ teaspoon (2.5 grams) baking powder
¼ teaspoon (1.25 grams) baking soda
1½ cups (180 grams) confectioners' sugar
¼ cup (60 grams) whole milk, room temperature

1. In a small saucepan, melt butter over medium-high heat. Cook, stirring frequently, until butter turns a medium-brown color and has a nutty aroma, about 10 minutes. Remove from heat, and pour into a heatproof bowl; let cool to room temperature and solidified. In a small microwave-safe bowl, reserve 2 tablespoons (28 grams) browned butter.
2. Preheat oven to 350°F (180°C). Line baking sheets with parchment paper.
3. In the bowl of a stand mixer fitted with the paddle attachment, beat brown sugar and remaining browned butter at medium speed until light and fluffy, 3 to 4 minutes, stopping to scrape paddle and bottom and sides of bowl. Beat in egg until well combined. Beat in vanilla.
4. In a medium bowl, whisk together flour, cornstarch, salt, baking powder, and baking soda. With mixer on low speed, gradually add flour mixture to sugar mixture, beating just until combined and stopping to scrape sides of bowl. Using a 1½-tablespoon (about 30 grams) spring-loaded scoop, scoop dough, and place 1½ inches apart on prepared pans.
5. Bake until edges are golden brown, 12 to 15 minutes. Let cool on pans for 5 minutes. Remove from pans, and let cool completely on wire racks.
6. Microwave reserved 2 tablespoons (28 grams) browned butter on high until melted; whisk in confectioners' sugar and milk until smooth and well combined. Drizzle onto cooled cookies. Let stand until glaze is set, about 1 hour. Store in an airtight container for up to 5 days.

Cinnamon Graham Crackers

Makes about 13 sheets/26 squares

A sprinkle of crunchy turbinado sugar on the outside gives way to the thick and slightly flaky interior of these graham crackers.

- **1 cup (227 grams) unsalted butter, softened**
- **½ cup (110 grams) firmly packed light brown sugar**
- **2 tablespoons (42 grams) molasses**
- **½ teaspoon (2 grams) vanilla extract**
- **1¾ cups (219 grams) all-purpose flour, plus more for dusting**
- **1 cup (125 grams) whole wheat flour**
- **1½ teaspoons (3 grams) ground cinnamon**
- **¾ teaspoon (3.75 grams) baking soda**
- **½ teaspoon (1.5 grams) kosher salt**
- **Turbinado sugar, for sprinkling**

1. In the bowl of a stand mixer fitted with the paddle attachment, beat butter and brown sugar at medium speed until creamy, 3 to 4 minutes, stopping to scrape paddle and bottom and sides of bowl. Beat in molasses and vanilla.

2. In a medium bowl, whisk together flours, cinnamon, baking soda, and salt. With mixer on low speed, gradually add flour mixture to butter mixture, beating until combined. Turn out dough onto a work surface, and shape into a rectangle. Wrap in plastic wrap, and refrigerate for 1 hour.

3. Preheat oven to 350°F (180°C). Line baking sheets with parchment paper.

4. Heavily dust work surface with all-purpose flour; on prepared surface, roll dough to ¼-inch thickness. Using a 2¼-inch square fluted cutter dipped in all-purpose flour, cut dough, rerolling scraps to use all dough. Place 2 dough pieces touching each other to create a sheet on a prepared pan. Repeat with remaining dough pieces, spacing 2 inches apart on prepared pans. Sprinkle with turbinado sugar.

5. Bake until edges are golden brown and centers are set, 17 to 20 minutes. Let cool on pans for 5 minutes. Remove from pans, and let cool completely on wire racks. Store in an airtight container for up to 1 week.

Pearl Sugar Ginger Cookies

Makes about 24 cookies

Pearl sugar lends gorgeous decoration and crunch to these fragrant cookies, and molasses in the dough helps them stay soft for days.

- ½ cup (113 grams) unsalted butter, softened
- ¾ cup (150 grams) granulated sugar
- ¼ cup (55 grams) firmly packed light brown sugar
- 1 teaspoon (3 grams) lemon zest
- ⅓ cup (113 grams) molasses (not blackstrap)
- 1 large egg (50 grams), room temperature
- 2¼ cups (281 grams) all-purpose flour
- 2 teaspoons (4 grams) ground ginger
- 1 teaspoon (5 grams) baking soda
- 1 teaspoon (3 grams) kosher salt
- ¾ teaspoon (1.5 grams) ground cinnamon
- ½ teaspoon (1 gram) ground cardamom
- ½ teaspoon (1 gram) ground cloves
- ½ cup (104 grams) Swedish pearl sugar

NOTE: *If pearl sugar isn't sticking as well, lightly dampen hands with water before rolling dough into balls and coating in sugar.*

1. Preheat oven to 350°F (180°C). Line 2 rimmed baking sheets with parchment paper.

2. In the bowl of a stand mixer fitted with the paddle attachment, beat butter, granulated sugar, brown sugar, and lemon zest at medium speed until fluffy, 2 to 3 minutes, stopping to scrape paddle and bottom and sides of bowl. Add molasses and egg; beat until well combined, stopping to scrape sides of bowl.

3. In a medium bowl, whisk together flour, ginger, baking soda, salt, cinnamon, cardamom, and cloves. Add flour mixture to butter mixture; beat at low speed until combined, stopping to scrape sides of bowl.

4. In a small shallow bowl, place pearl sugar.

5. Using a 1½-tablespoon (about 30 grams) spring-loaded scoop, scoop dough, and roll into balls. Roll dough balls in pearl sugar (see Note), and place 2 inches apart on prepared pans.

6. Bake, one pan at a time, until cookies appear cracked and edges are just set but centers look slightly underdone, about 10 minutes. Let cool on pan for 4 minutes. Remove from pan, and let cool completely on wire racks. Store in an airtight container for up to 1 week.

Pumpkin Cookies with Espresso Frosting

Makes about 16 cookies

Fall-apart tender with creamy pumpkin texture, these walk the line between cake and cookie.

- 2¼ cups (281 grams) all-purpose flour
- 2 teaspoons (4 grams) pumpkin pie spice
- 1½ teaspoons (3 grams) ground cinnamon
- 1 teaspoon (5 grams) baking soda
- 1 teaspoon (3 grams) kosher salt
- ¾ teaspoon (1 gram) instant espresso powder
- 1 cup (220 grams) firmly packed light brown sugar
- ⅔ cup (150 grams) unsalted butter, melted
- ⅔ cup (162 grams) canned pumpkin
- 1 large egg (50 grams), room temperature
- 1 teaspoon (4 grams) vanilla extract

Espresso Frosting (recipe follows)
Garnish: pumpkin pie spice

1. Preheat oven to 350°F (180°C). Line baking sheets with parchment paper.
2. In a medium bowl, whisk together flour, pie spice, cinnamon, baking soda, salt, and espresso powder.
3. In a large bowl, whisk together brown sugar, melted butter, pumpkin, egg, and vanilla. Gradually add flour mixture, stirring just until combined.
4. Using a 3-tablespoon (about 50 grams) spring-loaded scoop, scoop dough, and place 2 inches apart on prepared pans.
5. Bake, one pan at a time, until edges are set and tops are just set, 10 to 12 minutes. Let cool completely on pans on wire racks.
6. Using a small offset spatula, spread Espresso Frosting onto cooled cookies. Garnish with pie spice, if desired. Refrigerate in an airtight container for up to 3 days.

Espresso Frosting

Makes about 1¾ cups

- 1½ tablespoons (4 grams) instant espresso powder
- 1½ teaspoons (7.5 grams) water
- ¾ cup (170 grams) unsalted butter, softened
- 2 cups (240 grams) confectioners' sugar
- 1½ teaspoons (6 grams) vanilla extract
- ⅛ teaspoon kosher salt

1. In a small bowl, stir together espresso powder and 1½ teaspoons (7.5 grams) water until dissolved and well combined.
2. In the bowl of a stand mixer fitted with the paddle attachment, beat butter at medium speed until smooth and creamy, about 2 minutes, stopping to scrape sides of bowl. With mixer on low speed, gradually add confectioners' sugar, beating until combined. Add espresso mixture, vanilla, and salt; beat at medium speed until smooth and fluffy, about 2 minutes, stopping to scrape paddle and bottom and sides of bowl. Use immediately.

Pfeffernusse

Makes about 36 cookies

Pfeffernusse, or "peppernuts," originated in Germany and are very popular during the holidays. It's believed their name comes from the whole spices that are ground into powder to flavor the dough since traditional Pfeffernusse don't contain nuts, despite the name.

- **2¼ cups (281 grams) all-purpose flour**
- **1½ teaspoons (3 grams) ground ginger**
- **1½ teaspoons (3 grams) ground cinnamon**
- **½ teaspoon (2.5 grams) baking soda**
- **½ teaspoon (1.5 grams) kosher salt**
- **½ teaspoon (1 gram) ground cardamom**
- **½ teaspoon (1 gram) ground nutmeg**
- **½ teaspoon (1 gram) ground black pepper**
- **¼ teaspoon ground cloves**
- **⅓ cup (75 grams) unsalted butter**
- **⅓ cup (73 grams) firmly packed light brown sugar**
- **3 tablespoons (63 grams) unsulphured molasses**
- **3 tablespoons (63 grams) honey**
- **1 large egg (50 grams), room temperature and lightly beaten**
- **1½ cups (180 grams) confectioners' sugar**
- **2 tablespoons (30 grams) hot water (140°F/60°C to 150°F/66°C)**

1. In a medium bowl, whisk together flour, ginger, cinnamon, baking soda, salt, cardamom, nutmeg, pepper, and cloves.

2. In a medium saucepan, cook butter, brown sugar, molasses, and honey over medium heat, stirring frequently, until butter is melted, sugar dissolves, and bubbles form around sides of pan. Remove from heat, and pour mixture into a large heatproof bowl. Carefully stir in flour mixture until almost combined. Stir in egg until combined. (Mixture will be very soft and shiny.) Turn out dough onto plastic wrap, and flatten into a 6-inch square (about ¾ inch thick). Wrap in plastic wrap, and refrigerate until firm, at least 1 hour.

3. Preheat oven to 350°F (180°C). Line 2 baking sheets with parchment paper.

4. Cut dough into 1-inch-wide strips. Cut each strip crosswise into 1-inch pieces (about 16 grams each). Roll each piece into a ball. Place 1 inch apart on prepared pans.

5. Bake until set and edges are lightly browned, 12 to 15 minutes. Let cool on pans for 5 minutes. Remove from pans, and let cool completely on a wire rack.

6. Place a wire rack on a sheet of parchment paper.

7. In a small bowl, whisk together confectioners' sugar and 2 tablespoons (30 grams) hot water until smooth. Dip top of each cookie in glaze, and place on prepared rack, letting excess glaze drip off. Let stand until glaze is set, 45 minutes to 1 hour. Store in an airtight container for up to 5 days.

Chai Greek Wedding Cookies

Makes about 25 cookies

I updated the classic *kourabiedes* recipe by adding a touch of aromatic chai spice.

- 1 cup (227 grams) unsalted butter, softened
- 1¾ cups (210 grams) confectioners' sugar, divided
- 1 large egg yolk (19 grams)
- 1 tablespoon (15 grams) bourbon
- ½ teaspoon (2 grams) almond extract
- 2¾ cups (344 grams) all-purpose flour
- 2 teaspoons (4 grams) Chai Spice Mix (recipe follows)
- ½ teaspoon (2.5 grams) baking powder
- ½ teaspoon (1.5 grams) kosher salt

1. Preheat oven to 350°F (180°C). Line baking sheets with parchment paper.
2. In the bowl of a stand mixer fitted with the paddle attachment, beat butter at medium speed until smooth and creamy, 2 to 3 minutes, stopping to scrape paddle and bottom and sides of bowl. Add ¼ cup (30 grams) confectioners' sugar, and beat until well combined, about 1 minute. Beat in egg yolk. Slowly add bourbon and almond extract, beating until combined.
3. In a medium bowl, whisk together flour, Chai Spice Mix, baking powder, and salt. With mixer on low speed, gradually add flour mixture to butter mixture, beating just until combined and stopping to scrape paddle and bottom and sides of bowl. (Dough should be firm enough to shape but still soft.)
4. Divide dough into 25 portions (about 25 grams each). Roll each portion into a ball; roll each ball into a 3½-inch-long log. Shape each log into a "U," and place on prepared pans.
5. Bake until bottoms are lightly browned, 15 to 20 minutes. Let cool on pans for 5 minutes.
6. Line 2 baking sheets with parchment paper. Top 1 parchment-lined pan with a wire rack. Dust ½ cup (60 grams) confectioners' sugar onto other parchment-lined pan.
7. Place half of warm cookies on confectioners' sugar-dusted parchment; sift ½ cup (60 grams) confectioners' sugar onto cookies. Using a fork, push confectioners' sugar around cookies to cover any bare spots. Lift cookies with fork, tapping on edge of pan remove excess confectioners' sugar. Place on prepared rack, and let cool completely. Repeat procedure with remaining warm cookies and remaining ½ cup (60 grams) confectioners' sugar. Store in an airtight container for up to 4 days.

Chai Spice Mix

Makes about ⅓ cup

- 3 tablespoons (18 grams) ground cinnamon
- 4½ teaspoons (9 grams) ground ginger
- 1 tablespoon (6 grams) ground cloves
- 1½ teaspoons (3 grams) ground cardamom
- 1½ teaspoons (3 grams) finely ground black pepper

1. In a small bowl, stir together all ingredients. Store in an airtight container for up to 2 months.

Tiramisù Bars

Makes 24 bars

Featuring a buttery crust layered with a decadent mousse-like topping, these bars have the distinct flavors you love packed into perfectly sized portions.

- ⅓ cup (76 grams) unsalted butter, softened
- 1⅔ cups (333 grams) granulated sugar, divided
- 1 large egg (50 grams)
- 1½ teaspoons (6 grams) vanilla extract, divided
- 1½ cups (188 grams) all-purpose flour
- ½ teaspoon (2.5 grams) baking powder
- ½ teaspoon (1.5 grams) kosher salt
- 2 (8-ounce) containers (454 grams) mascarpone cheese, room temperature
- 2 cups (480 grams) cold heavy whipping cream
- 1 tablespoon (4 grams) instant espresso powder
- 1 tablespoon (15 grams) water
- 2 teaspoons (4 grams) unsweetened cocoa powder, plus more for dusting

Pro Tip

For clean edges to your bars, dip the blade of your knife into hot water and dry it between each cut.

1. Preheat oven to 350°F (180°C). Line a 13x9-inch baking pan with foil, letting excess extend over sides of pan; spray with baking spray with flour.

2. In the bowl of a stand mixer fitted with the paddle attachment, beat butter and ⅔ cup (133 grams) sugar at medium speed until light and fluffy, 3 to 4 minutes, stopping to scrape paddle and bottom and sides of bowl. Beat in egg and ½ teaspoon (2 grams) vanilla until combined; scrape paddle and bottom and sides of bowl.

3. In a medium bowl, whisk together flour, baking powder, and salt. With mixer on low speed, gradually add flour mixture to butter mixture, beating just until combined. Press mixture into bottom of prepared pan.

4. Bake until edges are golden brown and surface is dry and set, about 13 minutes. Let cool completely in pan on a wire rack.

5. Clean bowl of stand mixer. Using the whisk attachment, beat mascarpone and remaining 1 cup (200 grams) sugar at medium speed until smooth and sugar dissolves, 1 to 2 minutes. Add cold cream in a slow, steady stream, beating until combined. Beat in remaining 1 teaspoon (4 grams) vanilla. Thoroughly scrape whisk and bottom and sides of bowl. Slowly increase mixer speed to high, and beat until stiff peaks form, 1 to 2 minutes. Transfer half of mixture (about 3½ cups or 560 grams) to a medium bowl.

6. In a small bowl, whisk together espresso powder and 1 tablespoon (15 grams) water until smooth. Carefully fold espresso mixture and cocoa into one portion of mascarpone mixture.

7. Using an offset spatula, spread espresso mixture onto cooled crust. Freeze until just set, about 20 minutes. Spread remaining mascarpone mixture onto espresso mixture. Cover with plastic wrap, and freeze until firm and set, at least 2 hours, or up to overnight.

8. Using excess foil as handles, remove from pan, and cut into bars. Dust with cocoa. Let stand at room temperature for 20 to 30 minutes before serving. Refrigerate in an airtight container for up to 3 days.

Stollen Bites

Makes about 30 cookies

This iteration of the beloved fruit bread captures all the magic of traditional stollen but in bite-size form. Marzipan ensures the cookies stay moist, sweet, and tender, and the sweet tang of candied citrus peel complements the rich dried fruit, fragrant spices, and crunchy nuts.

- ⅓ cup (43 grams) raisins
- ¼ cup (32 grams) chopped dried apricots
- ¼ cup (32 grams) dried cherries
- ½ cup (120 grams) spiced rum or brandy
- ½ cup (120 grams) warm whole milk (105°F/41°C to 110°F/43°C), divided
- 1½ teaspoons (4.5 grams) active dry yeast
- 2 cups plus 1 tablespoon (258 grams) all-purpose flour, divided, plus more for dusting
- ½ cup (113 grams) plus ⅓ cup (75 grams) unsalted butter, melted and divided
- 1 large egg yolk (19 grams)
- 2 tablespoons (24 grams) granulated sugar, plus more for coating
- 1½ teaspoons (3 grams) orange zest
- ½ teaspoon (1.5 grams) kosher salt
- ½ teaspoon (1 gram) ground cinnamon
- ¼ teaspoon ground mace or nutmeg
- ¼ teaspoon ground cardamom
- ¼ teaspoon ground ginger
- 1 cup (135 grams) chopped mixed candied lemon and orange peel
- ⅓ cup (38 grams) slivered almonds, chopped
- 8 ounces (226 grams) marzipan (see Note)

Confectioners' sugar, for coating

1. In a medium bowl, combine raisins, apricots, cherries, and rum or brandy. Cover and let stand at least overnight or for up to 3 days. (The longer it stands, the stronger the flavor.)

2. In the bowl of a stand mixer, stir together ¼ cup (60 grams) warm milk and yeast by hand. Let stand until foamy, about 10 minutes.

3. Add ½ cup (63 grams) flour to yeast mixture, and stir with a wooden spoon or spatula until a smooth dough forms. Cover and let rise in a warm, draft-free place (75°F/24°C) until doubled in size, about 30 minutes.

4. Add ⅓ cup (75 grams) melted butter, egg yolk, granulated sugar, orange zest, salt, cinnamon, mace or nutmeg, cardamom, ginger, remaining 1½ cups plus 1 tablespoon (195 grams) flour, and remaining ¼ cup (60 grams) warm milk to yeast mixture; using the paddle attachment, beat at low speed until combined, about 2 minutes, stopping to scrape sides of bowl. Switch to the dough hook attachment, and beat at low speed until a smooth dough forms, 15 to 18 minutes.

5. Spray a large bowl with cooking spray. Place dough in bowl, turning to grease top. Cover and let rise in a warm, draft-free place (75°F/24°C) until doubled in size, about 1 hour.

6. Punch down dough in center; turn out onto a lightly floured surface.

7. Strain fruit mixture, discarding any liquid. Knead fruit mixture, candied peel, and almonds into dough until evenly dispersed. (Be patient while kneading. If any fruit or nut pieces fall out, just add them back to dough, and keep kneading.) Cover and let stand for 10 minutes.

8. Line baking sheets with parchment paper.

9. Divide dough into 30 portions (about 30 grams each). On a lightly floured surface, flatten 1 dough portion, and place ½ tablespoon (7 grams) marzipan in center. Wrap dough around marzipan, pinching to seal. With seam side down, shape dough into a ball; place on a prepared pan. Repeat with remaining dough and remaining marzipan, and place 2 inches apart on prepared pans. Cover and let rise in a warm, draft-free place (75°F/24°C) until puffed, about 45 minutes.

NOTE: *Be sure you're using marzipan and not almond paste for this recipe; marzipan is smoother and sweeter than almond paste, and the products are not interchangeable.*

10. Preheat oven to 350°F (180°C).

11. Bake until golden brown, a wooden pick inserted in center comes out clean, and an instant-read thermometer inserted near center registers 190°F (88°C), 15 to 18 minutes. Generously brush hot stollen with remaining ½ cup (113 grams) melted butter. Place stollen, one at a time, in a medium bowl, and dredge in granulated sugar to coat. Return to pans, and let cool completely.

12. Dredge cooled stollen in confectioners' sugar to coat. Store in an airtight container for up to 1 week. Dust with confectioners' sugar once more before serving, if desired.

Marbled Ginger Cookies

Makes about 12 cookies

The striking marble effect looks stunning and enhances the flavor experience, making these cookies a standout for both their taste and visual appeal. Each bite delivers a delightful blend of chewy and soft textures with subtle sweetness and spice.

- **¾ cup (170 grams) unsalted butter, softened**
- **1 cup (200 grams) granulated sugar, plus more for rolling**
- **¼ cup (55 grams) firmly packed light brown sugar**
- **1 large egg (50 grams), room temperature**
- **2 teaspoons (8 grams) vanilla extract**
- **2¼ cups (281 grams) plus 2 tablespoons (16 grams) all-purpose flour, divided**
- **1 teaspoon (5 grams) baking soda**
- **1 teaspoon (2 grams) ground ginger**
- **½ teaspoon (2.5 grams) baking powder**
- **2 tablespoons (42 grams) unsulphured molasses**
- **½ teaspoon (1 gram) ground cinnamon**
- **½ teaspoon (1 gram) Chinese five-spice powder**

1. Preheat oven to 350°F (180°C). Line baking sheets with parchment paper.

2. In the bowl of a stand mixer fitted with the paddle attachment, beat butter and sugars at medium speed until light and fluffy, 2 to 3 minutes, stopping to scrape paddle and bottom and sides of bowl. Beat in egg and vanilla until well combined.

3. In a medium bowl, whisk together 2¼ cups (281 grams) flour, baking soda, ginger, and baking powder. With mixer on low speed, gradually add flour mixture to butter mixture, beating until just combined. Transfer half of dough (about 395 grams) to a medium bowl. Add molasses to remaining dough in mixer bowl, and beat at low speed until combined.

4. In a small bowl, whisk together cinnamon, five-spice powder, and remaining 2 tablespoons (16 grams) flour. With mixer on low speed, gradually add cinnamon mixture to molasses dough, beating until just combined.

5. Using a 1½-tablespoon spring-loaded scoop, scoop doughs, and place on prepared pans. Using your hands, gently press 1 ball of each dough flavor together, and roll in your hands to create a swirl. Roll ball in granulated sugar, and place 2 inches apart on prepared pans. Repeat with remaining dough.

6. Bake until edges are set and centers are just barely puffed, 10 to 13 minutes. Let cool completely on pans on wire racks. Store in an airtight container for up to 1 week.

Nutty and Crunchy

These treats perfectly blend nuts, seeds, and other toothsome textures to create craving-conquering combos that are both familiar and surprising

Salted Popcorn Shortbread

Makes about 24 cookies

Inspired by childhood traditions of creating popcorn garland, as well as feasting on the giant tins of popcorn that come around during the holidays, this recipe gives a new and delicious way to use the crunchy-munchy snack in your seasonal baking.

- **2 cups (20 grams) popped plain popcorn**
- **1 cup (227 grams) unsalted butter, softened**
- **½ cup (100 grams) granulated sugar**
- **1 large egg yolk (19 grams), room temperature**
- **2 teaspoons (8 grams) vanilla extract**
- **1½ cups (188 grams) all-purpose flour, plus more for dusting**
- **½ teaspoon (1.5 grams) kosher salt**

1. In the work bowl of a food processor, pulse popcorn until finely crumbled.
2. In the bowl of a stand mixer fitted with the paddle attachment, beat butter and sugar at medium speed until light and creamy, 2 to 3 minutes, stopping to scrape paddle and bottom and sides of bowl. Add egg yolk, beating until combined. Beat in vanilla.
3. In a medium bowl, whisk together popcorn crumbs, flour, and salt. With mixer on low speed, gradually add popcorn mixture to butter mixture, beating until a soft dough forms, stopping to scrape paddle and bottom and sides of bowl. Wrap dough tightly in plastic wrap, and refrigerate for at least 30 minutes or up to overnight. (If refrigerating for longer than 30 minutes, let dough stand at room temperature for 5 minutes before rolling.)
4. Preheat oven to 350°F (180°C). Line baking sheets with parchment paper.
5. On a lightly floured surface, roll dough to ¼-inch thickness. Using a 2½-inch round cutter, cut dough, and place 2 inches apart on prepared pans. Reroll scraps and cut to use all dough.
6. Bake until edges are golden brown, 13 to 15 minutes. Let cool on pans for 10 minutes. Remove from pans, and let cool completely on wire racks. Store in an airtight container for up to 3 days.

Chocolate-Covered Crispy Rice Cookies

Makes about 18 cookies

A childhood favorite of mine, these soft, chewy cookies are full of nutty, sweet caramel and toasted crisp rice cereal, which is covered by a fudgy layer of melted milk chocolate. They're out of this world!

- **5 cups (150 grams) crisp rice cereal**
- **¼ cup (57 grams) unsalted butter, cubed**
- **½ cup (110 grams) firmly packed dark brown sugar**
- **½ cup (170 grams) light corn syrup**
- **3 tablespoons (120 grams) sweetened condensed milk**
- **1 teaspoon (7 grams) unsulphured molasses**
- **½ teaspoon (2 grams) vanilla extract**
- **¼ teaspoon kosher salt**
- **6 ounces (170 grams) milk chocolate melting wafers, melted according to package directions**

NOTE: *For the most classic shape, gently press on the edges of the disks after shaping with a cutter so they're slightly rounded.*

1. Preheat oven to 350°F (180°C). Line 2 rimmed baking sheets with parchment paper.
2. Spread cereal in an even layer on 1 prepared pan.
3. Bake until lightly browned, about 10 minutes, stirring every 3 minutes. Let cool completely. Transfer cereal to a large bowl.
4. In a large saucepan, cook butter and brown sugar over medium heat, stirring frequently, until melted, 3 to 4 minutes. Stir in corn syrup, condensed milk, and molasses, and bring to a low boil. Cook, stirring occasionally, until mixture registers 235°F (112°C) on an instant-read or candy thermometer. Remove from heat; add vanilla and salt, and immediately pour onto cooled toasted cereal. Gently stir until cereal is evenly coated.
5. Using a 3-tablespoon (about 30 grams) spring-loaded scoop, scoop cereal mixture, and place 1 inch apart on prepared pans. Place a 2¾-inch round cutter around a scoop, and gently press into a disk. (This helps with uniformity; see Note.) Repeat with remaining scoops. Let cool completely, about 20 minutes.
6. Using forks, dip disks, one at a time, into melted chocolate to fully coat, letting excess drip off. Return to pans, and let stand until chocolate is fully set, about 1 hour. Store in an airtight container for up to 1 week.

Coconut Magic Bars

Makes 18 bars

Also known as Hello Dolly Bars, these nostalgic treats are easy to make and perfect for an afternoon pick-me-up.

- **¾ cup plus 2 tablespoons (198 grams) unsalted butter**
- **2¼ cups (293 grams) graham cracker crumbs**
- **⅓ cup (73 grams) firmly packed light brown sugar**
- **¼ teaspoon kosher salt**
- **1 (14-ounce) can (396 grams) sweetened condensed milk**
- **1¼ cups (105 grams) sweetened flaked coconut**
- **1 cup (113 grams) coarsely chopped pecans**
- **1 cup (170 grams) semisweet chocolate chips**

Garnish: flaked sea salt

1. Preheat oven to 350°F (180°C). Line a 9-inch square baking pan with foil, letting excess extend over sides of pan; spray foil with baking spray with flour.
2. In a small saucepan, melt butter over medium heat. Cook, stirring occasionally, until butter turns a golden brown color and has a nutty aroma, 5 to 6 minutes. Remove from heat, and let cool slightly.
3. In a medium bowl, stir together browned butter, graham cracker crumbs, brown sugar, and kosher salt until well combined and mixture holds together when pressed. Using the bottom of a small measuring cup, press mixture into bottom of prepared pan.
4. Bake until fragrant and dry to the touch, about 15 minutes. Leave oven on.
5. Pour condensed milk onto warm prepared crust. Sprinkle with half of coconut, half of pecans, and half of chocolate chips. Sprinkle with remaining coconut, remaining pecans, and remaining chocolate chips. Lightly press with a clean spatula to adhere. Garnish with sea salt, if desired.
6. Bake until fragrant and golden brown, 30 to 40 minutes. Garnish with sea salt, if desired. Let cool completely in pan on a wire rack. Refrigerate until firm, 1 to 2 hours.
7. Using excess foil as handles, remove from pan, and cut into 3x1½-inch bars. Store in an airtight container for up to 3 days.

Paradise Blondie Brownies

Makes about 18 brownies

Why choose between brownies and blondies when you can have both? These blondie-topped brownies are packed with island flavor.

Brownie layer:

- 2½ cups (500 grams) granulated sugar
- 1½ cups (340 grams) unsalted butter, melted
- ½ cup (110 grams) firmly packed light brown sugar
- 5 large eggs (250 grams), room temperature
- 1½ teaspoons (6 grams) vanilla extract
- 1¼ cups (156 grams) all-purpose flour
- 1¼ cups (106 grams) Dutch process cocoa powder, sifted
- 2 teaspoons (4 grams) espresso powder
- 1 teaspoon (3 grams) kosher salt

Blondie layer:

- 2 cups (440 grams) firmly packed light brown sugar
- ⅔ cup (150 grams) unsalted butter, melted
- 2 large eggs (100 grams), room temperature
- 1 teaspoon (4 grams) coconut extract
- 1 teaspoon (4 grams) vanilla extract
- 2 cups (250 grams) all-purpose flour
- 1 teaspoon (5 grams) baking powder
- ¾ teaspoon (2.25 grams) kosher salt
- ½ cup (67 grams) salted macadamia nuts, coarsely chopped and divided
- ½ cup (28 grams) unsweetened coconut flakes, lightly toasted and divided
- 4 ounces (113 grams) semisweet chocolate, coarsely chopped and divided

1. Preheat oven to 350°F (180°C). Line a 13x9-inch baking pan with parchment paper, letting excess extend over sides of pan.
2. For brownie layer: In the bowl of a stand mixer fitted with the whisk attachment, beat granulated sugar, melted butter, and brown sugar at medium speed until well combined, 1 to 2 minutes, stopping to scrape bottom and sides of bowl. Add eggs, one at a time, beating well after each addition. Beat in vanilla.
3. In a medium bowl, whisk together flour, cocoa, espresso powder, and salt. With mixer on low speed, gradually add flour mixture to butter mixture, beating just until combined, stopping to scrape whisk and bottom and sides of bowl. Spread batter into prepared pan.
4. Bake for 25 minutes.
5. Meanwhile, for blondie layer: Clean bowl of stand mixer and whisk attachment. Using the whisk attachment, beat brown sugar and melted butter at medium speed until well combined, 1 to 2 minutes, stopping to scrape sides of bowl. Add eggs, one at a time, beating well after each addition. Beat in extracts.
6. In a medium bowl, whisk together flour, baking powder, and salt. With mixer on low speed, gradually add flour mixture to butter mixture, beating just until combined and stopping to scrape whisk and bottom and sides of bowl. Stir in half of nuts, half of coconut, and 1 ounce (28 grams) chopped chocolate.
7. Remove brownie layer from oven. Drop heaping tablespoonfuls of blondie batter onto brown, and gently spread with an offset spatula. (It's OK if layers get swirled together some.)
8. Bake for 25 minutes. Sprinkle with remaining 3 ounces (85 grams) chocolate and remaining nuts, gently pressing to adhere. Loosely cover pan with foil, and bake until top is golden brown and a wooden pick inserted in center comes out with a few moist crumbs, 25 to 30 minutes more.
9. Sprinkle with remaining coconut. Let cool completely in pan on a wire rack. Using excess parchment as handles, remove from pan, and cut into bars. Store in an airtight container for up to 3 days.

Baklava Bars

Makes about 24 bars

Baklava has a captivating history spanning many cultures and regions, though its exact origins remain debated among historians. It's believed to have roots in the Assyrian Empire's kitchens in Mesopotamia around the 8th century BC. Modern baklava gained popularity during the Ottoman Empire's peak influence in the Middle East and Balkans. Over centuries, various cultures along ancient trade routes—Greeks, Persians, Arabs, and Turks—contributed to baklava's evolution, resulting in the diverse versions enjoyed today. These bars offer a delicious twist on the classic, with a cookie crust topped with spiced nuts, baked until golden and fragrant, and drizzled with honey-orange syrup. It's less labor-intensive than the traditional phyllo pastry-layered version and just as delightful!

Crust:
- **1 cup (227 grams) unsalted butter, softened**
- **¾ cup (165 grams) firmly packed light brown sugar**
- **1 teaspoon (2 grams) orange zest**
- **1½ teaspoons (6 grams) vanilla extract**
- **3 cups (375 grams) all-purpose flour**
- **¾ teaspoon (2.25 grams) kosher salt**
- **½ teaspoon (2.5 grams) baking soda**
- **½ teaspoon (1 gram) ground cinnamon**

Filling:
- **½ cup (110 grams) firmly packed light brown sugar**
- **⅓ cup (76 grams) unsalted butter, melted**
- **1 cup (113 grams) chopped pistachios**
- **⅓ cup (38 grams) sliced almonds**
- **½ teaspoon (1.5 grams) kosher salt**
- **½ teaspoon (1 gram) ground cinnamon**
- **¼ teaspoon ground nutmeg**

Topping:
- **¼ cup (85 grams) honey**
- **1 teaspoon (2 grams) orange zest**
- **¼ cup (60 grams) fresh orange juice**
- **¼ teaspoon kosher salt**

1. Preheat oven to 350°F (180°C). Spray a 13x9-inch baking pan with baking spray with flour. Line pan with parchment paper, letting excess extend over sides of pan.
2. For crust: In the bowl of a stand mixer fitted with the paddle attachment, beat butter, brown sugar, and orange zest at medium speed until creamy, 2 to 3 minutes, stopping to scrape paddle and bottom and sides of bowl. Beat in vanilla.
3. In a large bowl, whisk together flour, salt, baking soda, and cinnamon. With mixer on low speed, gradually add flour mixture to butter mixture, beating just until combined. Press dough into bottom of prepared pan.
4. Bake for 15 minutes. Leave oven on.
5. For filling: In a medium bowl, whisk together brown sugar and melted butter until light and fluffy, about 2 minutes. Stir in pistachios, almonds, salt, cinnamon, and nutmeg until well combined. Spread mixture onto crust.
6. Bake until filling is golden brown, 12 to 15 minutes. Let cool for 10 minutes.
7. For topping: In a small saucepan, bring all ingredients to a boil over medium heat. Cook, stirring occasionally, until thick and syrupy, 5 to 6 minutes. Gently pour all over filling in pan, and let cool completely on a wire rack.
8. Using excess parchment as handles, remove from pan, and cut into bars. Spoon any topping in pan onto bars when serving. Store in airtight container for up to 3 days.

Pistachio Amaretti Cookies

Makes 15 cookies

The beloved amaretto cookie originated in Italy centuries ago. These cookies typically include almond flour or paste, sugar, and egg whites and are often enhanced with almond extract or bitter almonds. This rendition retains the qualities of traditional amaretti while introducing finely ground pistachios for a distinct richness and subtle al dente texture.

---

7 ounces (198 grams) blanched almonds, lightly toasted
3 ounces (85 grams) pistachios, toasted
1¼ cups (250 grams) granulated sugar, divided
¾ cup (90 grams) confectioners' sugar, divided
1 teaspoon (3 grams) kosher salt
2 large egg whites (60 grams), room temperature
1½ teaspoons (6 grams) vanilla extract
¼ teaspoon (1 gram) almond extract
Green gel food coloring

Pro Tip

To toast nuts, heat them in a dry skillet over medium-low heat, shaking or stirring occasionally, until fragrant and lightly browned. Let them cool completely before using.

1. Preheat oven to 300°F (150°C). Line baking sheets with parchment paper.
2. In the work bowl of a food processor, pulse almonds, pistachios, and ¾ cup (150 grams) granulated sugar until nuts are finely ground, stopping to scrape sides of bowl. Add ¼ cup (30 grams) confectioners' sugar and salt; pulse until combined. Add egg whites, one at a time, pulsing until combined after each addition. Add extracts and food coloring as desired; pulse just until a dough forms.
3. In separate small bowls, place remaining ½ cup (100 grams) granulated sugar and remaining ½ cup (60 grams) confectioners' sugar.
4. Using a 1½-tablespoon (about 30 grams) spring-loaded scoop, scoop dough, and roll into balls. Roll dough balls in granulated sugar to coat; roll in confectioners' sugar to coat. Place 2 inches apart on prepared pans.
5. Bake, one pan at a time, until tops are cracked, bottoms are golden brown, and edges are just set, about 30 minutes, rotating pan halfway through baking. Let cool on pan for 5 minutes. Remove from pan, and let cool completely on wire racks. Store in an airtight container for up to 3 days.

Melomakarona

Makes about 24 cookies

Soft, chewy, and swathed in citrus-infused honey, these cookies embody Mediterranean flavors and traditions. Although *melomakarona* are typically shaped by hand, I've sped up the process by rolling out the dough and using a cutter.

Dough:
- **2 cups (250 grams) unbleached cake flour**
- **½ cup (80 grams) semolina flour**
- **1 tablespoon (3 grams) orange zest**
- **1 teaspoon (5 grams) baking powder**
- **¾ teaspoon (2.25 grams) kosher salt**
- **½ teaspoon (2.5 grams) baking soda**
- **½ teaspoon (1 gram) ground cinnamon**
- **¼ teaspoon ground nutmeg**
- **⅛ teaspoon ground cloves**
- **¼ cup (50 grams) granulated sugar**
- **¼ cup (56 grams) extra-virgin olive oil**
- **¼ cup (56 grams) neutral oil**
- **¼ cup (60 grams) fresh orange juice**
- **2 tablespoons (30 grams) cognac**
- **1 tablespoon (21 grams) honey**
- **2 teaspoons (8 grams) vanilla extract**

Syrup:
- **1½ cups (300 grams) granulated sugar**
- **⅔ cup (160 grams) water**
- **2 teaspoons (2 grams) orange zest**
- **¼ cup (60 grams) fresh orange juice**
- **1 cinnamon stick**
- **2 whole cloves**
- **¼ cup (85 grams) honey**

Topping:
- **¼ cup (28 grams) finely chopped toasted walnuts**
- **¼ teaspoon ground cinnamon**
- **⅛ teaspoon kosher salt**

1. For dough: In a medium bowl, whisk together flours, orange zest, baking powder, salt, baking soda, cinnamon, nutmeg, and cloves.
2. In a large bowl, whisk together sugar, oils, orange juice, cognac, honey, and vanilla. Stir in flour mixture until a soft dough forms. Cover with plastic wrap, and refrigerate for 1 hour.
3. For syrup: In a small heavy-bottomed saucepan, bring sugar, ⅔ cup (160 grams) water, orange zest and juice, cinnamon, and cloves to a boil over medium heat, stirring occasionally until sugar dissolves. Remove from heat, and stir in honey. Pour into a heatproof shallow dish, and let cool completely.
4. Preheat oven to 350°F (180°C). Line baking sheets with parchment paper. Top 1 parchment-lined pan with a wire rack.
5. On a work surface, roll dough into a ½-inch-thick circle. Using a 1¾-inch round cutter, cut dough, and gently shape into ovals. Place 1 inch apart on prepared pans. Using a fork, gently prick top of dough once or twice. Reroll scraps and repeat procedure to use all dough.
6. Bake until bottom edges are lightly browned, about 20 minutes.
7. Meanwhile, for topping: In a small bowl, whisk together walnuts, cinnamon, and salt.
8. Working in batches of about 6 cookies, using a slotted spatula, immediately remove hot cookies from pan, and place in cooled syrup, gently turning cookies to coat. Place cookies on prepared rack, and sprinkle with topping. Let cookies cool completely on rack. Store in an airtight container for up to 3 days.

Almond Frangipane Cookies

Makes about 18 cookies

I love frangipane, a creamy spread of ground almonds, butter, and eggs that can be baked into cakes, pies, and practically anything else you can think of. It's one of the most common and popular fillings for croissants, so I took inspiration from that epic combo to create this cookie with the same flavors but in a fraction of the time and a lot less effort. A sprinkle of sliced almonds on top provides just enough crunchy contrast to the soft and chewy cookie base.

2¼ cups (281 grams) all-purpose flour
1 cup (96 grams) blanched almond flour
¾ teaspoon (3.75 grams) baking powder
½ teaspoon (1.5 grams) kosher salt
¼ teaspoon (1.25 grams) baking soda
1¼ cups (275 grams) firmly packed light brown sugar
1 cup (227 grams) unsalted butter, melted and cooled slightly
¾ cup (150 grams) granulated sugar
2 large eggs (100 grams)
2 teaspoons (8 grams) vanilla extract
1 teaspoon (4 grams) almond extract
1½ cups (170 grams) sliced almonds
Garnish: confectioners' sugar

1. Line a baking sheet with parchment paper.
2. In a medium bowl, whisk together flours, baking powder, salt, and baking soda.
3. In another medium bowl, whisk together brown sugar, melted butter, and granulated sugar until well combined. Whisk in eggs and extracts until smooth. Stir in flour mixture until just combined and no dry streaks remain. (Dough will seem soft.)
4. In a small bowl, place almonds.
5. Using a 3-tablespoon (about 60 grams) spring-loaded scoop, scoop dough directly into almonds, and roll until fully coated, gently pressing to adhere. Place on prepared pan. Refrigerate until firm, 45 minutes to 1 hour.
6. Preheat oven to 350°F (180°C). Line baking sheets with parchment paper.
7. Place dough balls 2 inches apart on prepared pans.
8. Bake, one pan at a time, until edges are set and golden brown, 17 to 20 minutes. Let cool on pan for 10 minutes. Remove from pan, and let cool completely on wire racks. Garnish with confectioners' sugar, if desired. Store in an airtight container for up to 4 days.

Pecan Pinwheels

Makes about 24 cookies

Uniting the rich flavor of smooth butter and nutty pecans in one mesmerizing swirl, these cakey cookies are coated in sugar and finely chopped pecans for irresistible crunch. This slice-and-bake dough needs some time to chill before slicing, so it's the ultimate make-ahead treat.

- **1⅔ cups (208 grams) plus 1½ cups (188 grams) all-purpose flour, divided, plus more for dusting**
- **2 teaspoons (4 grams) ground cinnamon**
- **1½ teaspoons (4.5 grams) kosher salt, divided**
- **1 teaspoon (5 grams) baking powder, divided**
- **½ cup (57 grams) coarsely chopped pecans, toasted**
- **1 cup (226 grams) unsalted butter, softened and divided**
- **½ cup (110 grams) firmly packed light brown sugar**
- **3 large eggs (150 grams), divided**
- **2½ teaspoons (10 grams) vanilla extract, divided**
- **½ cup (100 grams) granulated sugar**
- **½ cup (57 grams) finely chopped pecans**
- **¼ cup (50 grams) turbinado sugar**

Pro Tip

A bit of flour absorbs oils from the nuts and helps prevent a nut butter from forming in the food processor.

1. In a medium bowl, whisk together 1½ cups (188 grams) flour, cinnamon, 1 teaspoon (3 grams) salt, and ½ teaspoon (2.5 grams) baking powder.
2. In the work bowl of a food processor, pulse pecan pieces and 2 tablespoons flour mixture until pecans are finely ground, stopping to scrape sides of bowl. Whisk pecan mixture into remaining flour mixture until combined.
3. In the bowl of a stand mixer fitted with the paddle attachment, beat ½ cup (113 grams) butter and brown sugar at medium speed until creamy, 2 to 3 minutes, stopping to scrape paddle and bottom and sides of bowl. Add 1 egg (50 grams) and 1 teaspoon (4 grams) vanilla, beating until combined. With mixer on low speed, gradually add flour-pecan mixture to butter mixture, beating until combined, stopping to scrape paddle and bottom and sides of bowl. Turn out dough onto a lightly floured surface, and shape into a rectangle. Wrap in plastic wrap, and refrigerate for at least 1 hour.
4. Clean bowl of stand mixer and paddle attachment. Using the paddle attachment, beat granulated sugar and remaining ½ cup (113 grams) butter at medium speed until creamy, 2 to 3 minutes, stopping to scrape paddle and bottom and sides of bowl. Add 1 egg (50 grams) and remaining 1½ teaspoons (6 grams) vanilla, beating until combined.
5. In a medium bowl, whisk together remaining 1⅔ cups (208 grams) flour, remaining ½ teaspoon (1.5 grams) salt, and remaining ½ teaspoon (2.5 grams) baking powder. With mixer on low speed, gradually add flour mixture to sugar mixture, beating until combined and stopping to scrape paddle and bottom and sides of bowl. Turn out dough onto a lightly floured surface, and shape into a rectangle. Wrap in plastic wrap, and refrigerate until firm, at least 1 hour.
6. Let doughs stand at room temperature until slightly softened, about 5 minutes. On a lightly floured sheet of parchment paper, roll vanilla dough into a 14x10-inch rectangle (about ⅛ inch thick). Transfer dough on parchment to a baking sheet. Repeat procedure with pecan dough. Refrigerate for 15 minutes.
7. Transfer vanilla dough on parchment to a flat surface. Carefully invert pecan dough onto vanilla dough. With parchment still on pecan dough, gently roll doughs a few times to press together. Remove top sheet of parchment. Starting at one long side, slowly but tightly roll doughs together into a log, using bottom sheet of parchment to help lift and roll. (If dough cracks, stop rolling, and

let stand for a few minutes until pliable.) Tightly wrap in parchment paper, twisting ends of parchment to seal. Place, seam side down, on a baking sheet. Refrigerate until firm, at least 2 hours.

8. Preheat oven to 325°F (170°C). Line baking sheets with parchment paper.

9. In a wide, shallow dish, whisk together chopped pecans and turbinado sugar. In a small bowl, whisk remaining 1 egg (50 grams); brush onto dough log. Roll dough in pecan sugar to coat, gently pressing to adhere. Using a sharp knife, cut log into ½-inch-thick slices. Place 1 inch apart on prepared pans.

10. Bake until edges are lightly brown, 12 to 14 minutes, rotating pans halfway through baking. Let cool completely on pans on wire racks. Store in an airtight container for up to 1 week.

Toasted Hazelnut Sablés

Makes about 22 cookies

European-style butter makes these sparkling sablés a decadent, melt-in-your-mouth experience.

- **⅓ cup (38 grams) whole peeled hazelnuts, toasted**
- **2 cups (250 grams) all-purpose flour**
- **¾ cup plus 2 tablespoons (198 grams) unsalted European-style butter, softened**
- **⅓ cup (40 grams) confectioners' sugar**
- **1¼ cups (250 grams) granulated sugar, divided**
- **1 teaspoon (3 grams) kosher salt**
- **1 vanilla bean, split lengthwise, seeds scraped and reserved**
- **1 large egg yolk (19 grams)**

1. In the work bowl of a food processor, pulse toasted hazelnuts until finely ground, stopping to scrape sides of bowl. In a medium bowl, whisk together ground nuts and flour.
2. In the bowl of a stand mixer fitted with the paddle attachment, beat butter at medium-low speed until smooth, about 1 minute. Add confectioners' sugar, ¼ cup (50 grams) granulated sugar, and salt, and beat until smooth, about 1 minute, stopping to scrape paddle and bottom and sides of bowl. Add reserved vanilla seeds and egg yolk, and beat until combined, about 1 minute. Add flour mixture in two additions, beating just until combined after each addition and stopping to scrape paddle and bottom and sides of bowl. Turn out dough onto a work surface, and gently knead 3 to 4 times.
3. Place dough between 2 sheets of parchment paper, and roll to ½-inch thickness. Transfer dough between parchment to refrigerator. Refrigerate until set, at least 2 hours.
4. Preheat oven to 325°F (170°C). Line baking sheets with parchment paper.
5. Using a 2-inch round cutter dipped in flour, cut dough, and place 1 inch apart on prepared pans. Repeat rerolling scraps, refrigerating, and cutting to use all dough.
6. Bake, one pan at a time, until bottom edges are golden brown, about 15 minutes. Let cool on pans for 1 minute.
7. In a shallow dish, place remaining 1 cup (200 grams) granulated sugar. Using a spatula, place a few cookies at a time in sugar; use a small spoon to cover top and sides with sugar. Using spatula, lift cookies, and let cool completely on wire racks. Store in an airtight container for up to 5 days.

Baci di Alassio

Makes 24 to 30 sandwich cookies

Similar to a macaron but with a little more textured crunch from ground hazelnuts, *baci di Alassio*, or "kisses of Alassio," are a regional Italian confection native to Alassio, a town in the province of Savona situated on the western coast of Liguria in Northern Italy. I filled these sweet kisses with a chocolate-hazelnut ganache that beautifully bolsters their flavor.

- **¼ cup (43 grams) finely chopped semisweet chocolate**
- **¼ cup (77 grams) hazelnut chocolate spread**
- **3 tablespoons (45 grams) heavy whipping cream**
- **14 ounces (400 grams) roasted unsalted whole hazelnuts (about 3 cups)**
- **⅔ cup (134 grams) granulated sugar, divided**
- **¼ cup (21 grams) sifted Dutch process cocoa powder**
- **½ teaspoon (1.5 grams) kosher salt**
- **½ teaspoon (1 gram) instant espresso powder**
- **3 large egg whites (90 grams), room temperature**
- **1 tablespoon (21 grams) clover honey**
- **½ teaspoon (3 grams) vanilla bean paste**

NOTES: *If desired, use a permanent marker to draw 1¼- to 1½-inch circles 1 inch apart onto 2 sheets of parchment paper. Place paper with marker side down on baking sheets. Silicone macaron baking mats with sized circles can also be used as a guide.*

Cooled cookies can have a shiny or matte finish, depending on several factors, but will be delicious all the same.

1. In the top of a double boiler, cook chocolate, hazelnut chocolate spread, and cream over simmering water, stirring frequently, until chocolate is melted and mixture is smooth and well combined. Remove from heat, and let stand at room temperature, whisking occasionally, until thickened, about 1 hour.

2. Preheat oven to 375°F (190°C). Line baking sheets with parchment paper.

3. In the work bowl of a food processor, pulse hazelnuts, ⅓ cup (67 grams) sugar, cocoa, salt, and espresso powder until hazelnuts are very finely ground, stopping to scrape sides of bowl.

4. In the bowl of a stand mixer fitted with the whisk attachment, beat egg whites at medium-high speed until foamy. With mixer on medium-high, gradually add remaining ⅓ cup (67 grams) sugar in a slow, steady stream, beating until stiff peaks form. Fold in hazelnut-sugar mixture in three additions just until combined. Fold in honey and vanilla bean paste until well combined.

5. Spoon hazelnut mixture into a pastry bag fitted with a ½-inch open star piping tip (Ateco #826). Pipe 1¼- to 1½-inch-wide rosettes or kisses on prepared pans (see Notes); gently pat down or smooth any rough piped ends, if needed. Alternatively, divide dough into 2-teaspoon (about 12-gram) portions; shape each into 1¼- to 1½-inch-wide disks (about ¼ inch thick).

6. Bake, one pan at a time, until cookies look dry and set but are still slightly soft to the touch, 10 to 12 minutes. Let cool completely on pan on a wire rack. (See Notes.)

7. Stir thickened cooled chocolate-hazelnut mixture. Spoon into a pastry bag; cut a ¼-inch opening in tip. Pipe onto flat side of half of cooled cookies. Top with remaining cookies, flat side down. Refrigerate until filling is set before serving, about 20 minutes. Refrigerate in an airtight container for up to 3 days.

Chocolate-Hazelnut Filled Biscotti

Makes 22 to 24 biscotti

This twist on the traditional Italian biscuit is perfect for folks who crave a cookie with crunch for days. They're a particularly good accompaniment to cappuccino, another Italian favorite.

½ cup (113 grams) unsalted butter, softened
⅓ cup (67 grams) granulated sugar
¼ cup (55 grams) firmly packed light brown sugar
2 large eggs (100 grams), room temperature
1 teaspoon (6 grams) vanilla bean paste
½ teaspoon (2 grams) almond extract
2¼ cups (281 grams) all-purpose flour, plus more for dusting
1 teaspoon (5 grams) baking powder
1 teaspoon (3 grams) kosher salt
½ cup (154 grams) hazelnut chocolate spread
3 tablespoons (24 grams) very finely chopped dry-roasted unsalted hazelnuts
Hazelnut Chocolate Glaze (recipe follows)
Garnish: chopped dry-roasted hazelnuts

NOTE: *This recipe produces crisp biscotti. If you prefer yours with a softer texture, the second bake in step 9 can be for a shorter period of time.*

1. Preheat oven to 325°F (170°C). Line a large baking sheet with parchment paper.
2. In the bowl of a stand mixer fitted with the paddle attachment, beat butter and sugars at medium speed until fluffy, about 3 minutes, stopping to scrape paddle and bottom and sides of bowl. Beat in eggs, vanilla bean paste, and almond extract. (Mixture may look a bit broken, but dough will come together.)
3. In a medium bowl, whisk together flour, baking powder, and salt. With mixer on low speed, gradually add flour mixture to butter mixture, beating until combined and stopping to scrape paddle and bottom and sides of bowl.
4. Divide dough in half, and shape each portion of dough into a 6½x5-inch rectangle. (Keep one portion dough covered to prevent it from drying out.) Place 1 dough rectangle on a lightly floured sheet of parchment paper, and lightly flour top of dough; place another sheet of parchment on top of dough. Roll dough between parchment into a 12x8-inch rectangle, lightly flouring dough as needed to prevent sticking. Remove top parchment.
5. Using a small offset spatula, spread half of hazelnut chocolate spread onto dough, leaving a ½-inch border around edges. Sprinkle with half of very finely chopped hazelnuts. Starting on one short side and using parchment to help support, roll up dough into a log. Pinch ends to seal, and tuck edges under to create a rectangular block about 1 inch tall. Place dough, seam side down, on prepared pan.
6. Repeat procedure with remaining dough, remaining hazelnut chocolate spread, and remaining very finely chopped hazelnuts. Space dough blocks 3 to 4 inches apart on prepared pan.
7. Bake until golden brown and edges are set, 35 to 40 minutes. (Dough will crack a little along the top; this is OK.) Let cool on pan for 10 minutes. Leave oven on.
8. Carefully transfer rectangles to a cutting board. Using a serrated knife, carefully cut rectangles crosswise into ¾-inch-thick slices. Place slices, cut side down, 1 inch apart on pan.
9. Bake until toasted and centers are mostly dry and firm, 30 to 37 minutes (see Note), turning biscotti halfway through baking. Remove from pan, and let cool completely on a wire rack.
10. Drizzle or spread Hazelnut Chocolate Glaze onto cooled biscotti. Garnish with chopped hazelnuts, if desired. Let stand until glaze is set, about 30 minutes. Store in an airtight container for up to 3 days.

Hazelnut Chocolate Glaze

Makes about ⅔ cup

1 cup (120 grams) confectioners' sugar, sifted
2 tablespoons (30 grams) water
⅛ teaspoon kosher salt
¼ cup (77 grams) hazelnut chocolate spread

1. In a small bowl, whisk together confectioners' sugar, 2 tablespoons (30 grams) water, anc salt until well combined. Whisk in hazelnut chocolate spread until smooth and well combined. Use immediately.

Chocolate Chunk, Toffee, and Pomegranate Cookie Bars

Makes 18 bars

Chock-full of buttery toffee, rich chocolate, and tart pomegranate, these bars are a lesson in balancing decadent sweetness with fruity tang.

- 2¼ cups (281 grams) all-purpose flour
- 1½ teaspoons (4.5 grams) cornstarch
- 1 teaspoon (5 grams) baking soda
- ½ teaspoon (1.5 grams) kosher salt
- 1 cup (166 grams) pomegranate arils
- 1 cup (220 grams) firmly packed light brown sugar
- ¾ cup (170 grams) unsalted butter, melted
- ¼ cup (50 grams) granulated sugar
- 1 large egg (50 grams)
- 1 large egg yolk (19 grams)
- 2 teaspoons (8 grams) vanilla extract
- ¾ cup (128 grams) semisweet chocolate chunks
- ¾ cup (122 grams) toffee bits
- Flaked sea salt, for sprinkling
- Pomegranate Glaze (recipe follows)

1. Preheat oven to 350°F (180°C). Lightly spray a 9-inch square baking pan with cooking spray. Line pan with parchment paper, letting excess extend over sides.
2. In a large bowl, whisk together flour, cornstarch, baking soda, and kosher salt; stir in pomegranate arils.
3. In a medium bowl, whisk together brown sugar, melted butter, and granulated sugar. Whisk in egg, egg yolk, and vanilla until smooth. Stir sugar mixture into flour mixture until dry ingredients are moistened; stir in chocolate and toffee until well combined. Spread dough into prepared pan.
4. Bake until golden brown and set, about 35 minutes. Sprinkle with sea salt. Let cool completely in pan on a wire rack.
5. Using excess parchment as handles, remove from pan, and cut into bars. Drizzle with Pomegranate Glaze before serving. Store in an airtight container for up to 3 days.

Pomegranate Glaze

Makes about 1 cup

- 1 cup (120 grams) confectioners' sugar
- 2 tablespoons (42 grams) pomegranate molasses (see Note)
- 1 tablespoon (15 grams) heavy whipping cream

1. In a small bowl, whisk together all ingredients until combined. Use immediately.

NOTE: *Pomegranate molasses is easily found online and at specialty food stores.*

Feel-Good Favorites

Baked with nostalgia, these beloved classics—like glazed animal crackers and shopping-mall-store giant cookie cakes—rekindle sweet memories from the past

Iced Animal Crackers

Makes about 60 cookies

These cookies are virtually identical to my childhood favorite brand of animal cookies. The thin glaze of royal icing settles into the imprints of the design and dries to a crisp finish that makes the shapes pop.

½ cup (113 grams) unsalted butter, softened
¼ cup (50 grams) granulated sugar
2 tablespoons (42 grams) honey
1 large egg (50 grams), room temperature
1¼ teaspoons (5 grams) vanilla extract, divided
¾ cup (94 grams) all-purpose flour, plus more for dusting
¾ cup (94 grams) whole wheat flour
1 teaspoon (5 grams) baking powder
¾ teaspoon (1.5 grams) ground cinnamon
½ teaspoon (1.5 grams) kosher salt
1 cup (120 grams) confectioners' sugar
1 teaspoon (5 grams) meringue powder
2 tablespoons (30 grams) water
Pale pink gel food coloring

1. Preheat oven to 350°F (180°C). Line baking sheets with parchment paper.

2. In the bowl of a stand mixer fitted with the paddle attachment, beat butter, granulated sugar, and honey at medium speed until well combined, stopping to scrape paddle and bottom and sides of bowl. Add egg and 1 teaspoon (4 grams) vanilla; beat until combined.

3. In a medium bowl, whisk together flours, baking powder, cinnamon, and salt. With mixer on low speed, gradually add flour mixture to butter mixture, beating until just combined and no dry streaks remain, stopping to scrape paddle and bottom and sides of bowl.

4. Lightly dust work surface with all-purpose flour; on prepared surface, roll dough to ¼-inch thickness. Using assorted 2-inch animal-shaped cutters, cut dough, and place 1 inch apart on prepared pans.

5. Bake until edges are set and surface is dry, 8 to 10 minutes. Let cool on pans for 10 minutes. Remove from pans, and let cool completely on wire racks.

6. In a small bowl, whisk together confectioners' sugar and meringue powder; whisk in 2 tablespoons (30 grams) water and remaining ¼ teaspoon (1 gram) vanilla until smooth. Pour half of mixture into another small bowl, and tint with food coloring as desired. Using a pastry brush or a small food-safe paintbrush, brush a thin layer of glaze onto cookies as desired. Let stand until glaze is dry, at least 2 hours, or up to overnight. Store in an airtight container for up to 1 week.

Skillet Sprinkle Sugar Cookie

Makes 1 (10-inch) cookie

This giant sugar cookie will fill you with childhood nostalgia.

---

1 cup (227 grams) unsalted butter, softened
½ cup (100 grams) granulated sugar
½ cup (110 grams) firmly packed light brown sugar
1 large egg (50 grams), room temperature
1 tablespoon (13 grams) vanilla extract
3¼ cups (406 grams) all-purpose flour
1 tablespoon (15 grams) baking powder
½ teaspoon (1.5 grams) kosher salt
⅓ cup plus 1 tablespoon (108 grams) rainbow sprinkles
Garnish: confectioners' sugar

1. Preheat oven to 350°F (180°C). Spray a 10-inch cast-iron skillet with baking spray with flour.
2. In the bowl of a stand mixer fitted with the paddle attachment, beat butter, granulated sugar, and brown sugar at medium speed until creamy, 2 to 3 minutes, stopping to scrape paddle and bottom and sides of bowl. Add egg and vanilla, beating well.
3. In a large bowl, whisk together flour, baking powder, and salt. Gradually add flour mixture to butter mixture, beating at low speed until combined, stopping to scrape paddle and bottom and sides of bowl. Fold in ⅓ cup sprinkles. Spread batter into prepared pan. Sprinkle remaining 1 tablespoon sprinkles onto batter.
4. Bake until a wooden pick inserted in center comes out clean, about 30 minutes. Let cool completely in pan on a wire rack. Cut into wedges. Garnish with confectioners' sugar, if desired. Store in an airtight container for up to 5 days.

Chocolate Chip Cookie Cake

Makes 1 (10-inch) cookie cake

I have fond memories of perusing all the colorfully decorated cookie cakes on display in my local mall's food court. My from-scratch take has the perfect soft and chewy texture just like the mall version, and the sweet swirls of buttercream decorating the edges will make you feel like a kid again at first bite.

- ¾ cup (170 grams) unsalted butter, melted
- ¾ cup (165 grams) firmly packed light brown sugar
- ½ cup (100 grams) granulated sugar
- 1 large egg (50 grams), room temperature
- 1 large egg yolk (19 grams), room temperature
- 1½ teaspoons (6 grams) vanilla extract
- 2 cups (250 grams) all-purpose flour
- 1 teaspoon (3 grams) kosher salt
- ½ teaspoon (2.5 grams) baking soda
- ¼ teaspoon (1.25 grams) baking powder
- ¾ cup (129 grams) coarsely chopped bittersweet chocolate
- Vanilla Buttercream (recipe follows)
- Garnish: finely chopped bittersweet chocolate

1. Preheat oven to 350°F (180°C). Spray a 10-inch round cake pan with baking spray with flour.
2. In a medium bowl, whisk together melted butter, sugars, egg, egg yolk, and vanilla extract until combined.
3. In another medium bowl, whisk together flour, salt, baking soda, and baking powder. Fold flour mixture into butter mixture until almost completely combined. Fold in coarsely chopped chocolate until combined and no dry streaks remain. Press dough into an even layer in prepared pan.
4. Bake until surface is dry and edges are lightly browned, 25 to 30 minutes. Let cool completely in pan on a wire rack. Remove from pan, and transfer to a serving platter.
5. Spoon Vanilla Buttercream into a pastry bag fitted with a small open star piping tip (Ateco #824). Pipe buttercream around edge of cooled cookie. Garnish with finely chopped chocolate, if desired. Store in an airtight container for up to 3 days.

Vanilla Buttercream

Makes about 2½ cups

- 1 cup (227 grams) unsalted butter, softened
- ½ teaspoon (1.5 grams) kosher salt
- 2½ cups (300 grams) confectioners' sugar
- 1 tablespoon (15 grams) heavy whipping cream
- 2 teaspoons (8 grams) vanilla extract

1. In the bowl of a stand mixer fitted with the paddle attachment, beat butter and salt at medium speed until smooth and creamy. With mixer on low speed, gradually add confectioners' sugar, beating until combined and stopping to scrape paddle and bottom and sides of bowl. Beat in cream and vanilla. Slowly increase mixer speed to high, and beat until pale and fluffy, 1 to 2 minutes, stopping to scrape paddle and bottom and sides of bowl. Use immediately.

Linzer Cookie Torte

Makes 1 (9½-inch) cookie

Linzer cookie dough is reimagined as a buttery, lightly spiced, and slightly citrusy crust, with a generous slathering of berry preserves spread throughout the middle for a classic jammy note. Topped with a cutout crust and dusted with confectioners' sugar, this torte is sure to impress.

---

1 cup (227 grams) unsalted butter, room temperature
⅔ cup (133 grams) granulated sugar
⅓ cup (73 grams) firmly packed light brown sugar
2 large eggs (100 grams), room temperature and divided
¾ teaspoon (4.5 grams) vanilla bean paste
½ teaspoon (1 gram) packed lemon zest
2½ cups (313 grams) all-purpose flour, plus more for dusting
½ cup (48 grams) hazelnut flour
1 teaspoon (2 grams) ground nutmeg
½ teaspoon (1.5 grams) kosher salt
1 cup (320 grams) seedless blackberry preserves
1 tablespoon (15 grams) water
Garnish: confectioners' sugar

1. In the bowl of a stand mixer fitted with the paddle attachment, beat butter, granulated sugar, and brown sugar at medium speed until creamy, 2 to 3 minutes, stopping to scrape paddle and bottom and sides of bowl. Beat in 1 egg (50 grams), vanilla bean paste, and lemon zest until well combined.
2. In a medium bowl, whisk together flours, nutmeg, and salt. With mixer on low speed, gradually add flour mixture to butter mixture, beating just until combined. Turn out onto a work surface lightly dusted with all-purpose flour, and divide dough in half (about 415 grams each). Shape each half into a disk, and wrap in plastic wrap. Refrigerate until firm, at least 2 hours, or up to overnight.
3. Spray a 9½-inch round fluted removable-bottom tart pan with baking spray with flour.
4. Lightly dust work surface with all-purpose flour; on prepared surface, roll half of dough into a 10-inch circle (about ½ inch thick). Gently transfer to prepared pan, pressing into bottom and ½ inch up sides. Spread preserves in prepared crust.
5. Lightly dust work surface with all-purpose flour; on prepared surface, roll remaining dough into a 10-inch circle (about ½ inch thick). Trim dough into a 9½-inch circle. Using 4-inch and 1-inch diamond cutters dipped in flour, cut center from dough in desired pattern. Using a rolling pin, transfer dough to top of preserves. Using a small knife, trim bottom crust to sit even with top crust. Freeze until firm, about 30 minutes.
6. Preheat oven to 350°F (180°C).
7. In a small bowl, whisk together 1 tablespoon (15 grams) water and remaining 1 egg (50 grams). Using a pastry brush, brush dough with egg wash.
8. Bake until top crust is dry and golden brown, 30 to 35 minutes. Let cool in pan for 15 minutes. Remove from pan, and let cool completely on a wire rack. Garnish with confectioners' sugar, if desired. Store in an airtight container for up to 3 days.

Cuccidati Cookie Cake

Makes 1 (9-inch) cookie cake

Filled with a lightly spiced fig and nut mixture, this is a delectable twist on the classic Italian rolled cookie.

Dough:
- 3 cups (375 grams) all-purpose flour, plus more for dusting
- ½ cup (100 grams) granulated sugar
- 2 teaspoons (6 grams) kosher salt
- 1½ teaspoons (7.5 grams) baking powder
- 1 cup (227 grams) unsalted butter, softened
- 2 large eggs (100 grams), room temperature
- 2 teaspoons (8 grams) vanilla extract

Filling:
- 1½ cups (210 grams) dried figs, stemmed and chopped
- ¼ cup plus 2 tablespoons (90 grams) water
- ¼ cup (85 grams) honey
- 1½ teaspoons (3 grams) orange zest
- ¼ cup (60 grams) fresh orange juice
- ¾ cup (105 grams) pitted dates, finely chopped
- ¾ cup (85 grams) chopped toasted walnuts
- ⅓ cup (43 grams) raisins
- 1 teaspoon (3 grams) kosher salt
- 1 teaspoon (2 grams) ground cinnamon
- ¼ teaspoon ground nutmeg
- ¼ teaspoon ground cloves

Glaze:
- 2 cups (240 grams) confectioners' sugar
- 3 tablespoons (45 grams) whole milk

Garnish: rainbow nonpareils

1. For dough: In the work bowl of a food processor, pulse flour, granulated sugar, salt, and baking powder until combined. Add butter, eggs, and vanilla; pulse just until a smooth dough forms. (Do not overprocess.)

2. Turn out dough onto a lightly floured surface, and knead for 2 to 3 minutes. Shape two-thirds of dough (about 544 grams) into a disk. Shape remaining one-third of dough (about 272 grams) into a disk. Wrap dough disks separately in plastic wrap, and refrigerate for at least 1 hour or up to overnight.

3. For filling: In a medium saucepan, cook figs, ¼ cup plus 2 tablespoons (90 grams) water, honey, and orange juice over medium heat, stirring occasionally, until figs are fork-tender, about 10 minutes. Transfer mixture to the work bowl of a food processor. Add orange zest, dates, walnuts, raisins, salt, cinnamon, nutmeg, and cloves, and process until smooth. Cover until ready to use.

4. Preheat oven to 350°F (180°C). Spray a 9-inch round cake pan with baking spray with flour. Line bottom of pan with parchment paper.

5. On a lightly floured surface, roll larger dough disk into a 13-inch circle. Carefully transfer to prepared pan, pressing into bottom and up sides of pan. (If dough breaks, press it together and smooth it out with your fingers.) Spread filling into prepared crust. Using a small paring knife, trim excess dough to ¼ inch above top of filling. Using your fingers, gently fold ¼-inch edge of dough over filling, and smooth down slightly with your fingertips.

6. On a lightly floured surface, roll remaining dough disk into a 10-inch circle. Using a sharp knife and a 9-inch round cake pan as a guide, cut dough into a 9-inch circle. Carefully place dough on filling. Using your fingers or a fork, lightly press down on edges of dough to seal. Using a fork or wooden pick, gently poke a few holes in top of dough.

7. Bake until top is lightly browned, 40 to 45 minutes. Let cool in pan for 10 minutes. Carefully remove from pan, and let cool completely on a wire rack.

8. For glaze: In a medium bowl, whisk together confectioners' sugar and milk until smooth; spread onto cooled cookie. Garnish with nonpareils, if desired. Let stand until glaze is set, 15 to 20 minutes. Store in an airtight container for up to 3 days.

Wedding Cake Cookie Layer Cake

Makes 1 (8-inch) cake

I've always loved a generously filled sandwich cookie, and I can always find a reason to celebrate—birthdays, anniversaries, weddings, Wednesdays—so why not celebrate by turning sandwich cookies into a layered cookie cake!

Wedding Cake Sandwich Cookies (recipe on page 68)
Wedding Cake Buttercream (recipe on page 68)
Garnish: rainbow sprinkles

1. Spray 2 (8-inch) round cake pans with baking spray with flour. Line bottom of pans with parchment paper.
2. Prepare Wedding Cake Sandwich Cookies through step 2. Divide dough between prepared pans (about 582 grams each), gently pressing dough into bottom of each pan. Refrigerate until firm, about 30 minutes.
3. Preheat oven to 350°F (180°C).
4. Bake until golden brown, 25 to 30 minutes. Let cool in pans for 10 minutes. Remove from pans, and let cool completely on wire racks.
5. Place 1 cooled cookie layer on a serving plate; spread ½ cup plus 2 tablespoons (about 175 grams) Wedding Cake Buttercream on top. Top with remaining cookie layer. Spread remaining buttercream on top and sides of cake to create a naked cake look. Garnish with sprinkles, if desired. Refrigerate until buttercream is firm before serving, 15 to 30 minutes. Store in an airtight container for up to 3 days.

Snickerdoodle Brookie

Makes 1 (9-inch) cookie cake

A brookie is a heavenly hybrid of a brownie and a cookie. But this Snickerdoodle Brookie is a new level of epic dessert mash-up. Cinnamon-scented cookie dough is blended with fudgy brownie batter to create a treat you never knew you wanted—until that first fantastic bite.

Brownie batter:

- 6 ounces (170 grams) bittersweet baking chocolate, finely chopped
- ½ cup (113 grams) unsalted butter, cubed
- 1 cup (200 grams) granulated sugar
- 2 large eggs (100 grams)
- 1 teaspoon (4 grams) vanilla extract
- ¾ cup (94 grams) all-purpose flour
- ¼ cup (21 grams) Dutch process cocoa powder
- ½ teaspoon (1.5 grams) kosher salt

Snickerdoodle dough:

- ⅓ cup (76 grams) unsalted butter, softened
- ½ cup (100 grams) granulated sugar
- 1 large egg (50 grams)
- ½ teaspoon (2 grams) vanilla extract
- 1 cup (125 grams) all-purpose flour
- ½ teaspoon (1.5 grams) kosher salt
- ½ teaspoon (1 gram) ground cinnamon
- ¼ teaspoon (1.25 grams) baking powder

Topping:

- 1 tablespoon (12 grams) granulated sugar
- ⅛ teaspoon ground cinnamon

1. Preheat oven to 350°F (180°C).
2. For brownie batter: In the top of a double boiler, heat chocolate and butter over simmering water, stirring occasionally, until melted and smooth. Remove from heat, and whisk in sugar. Let cool for 5 minutes; whisk in eggs and vanilla until well combined.
3. In a medium bowl, whisk together flour, cocoa, and salt. Fold flour mixture into chocolate mixture just until combined.
4. For snickerdoodle dough: In the bowl of a stand mixer fitted with the paddle attachment, beat butter and sugar at medium speed until fluffy, 3 to 4 minutes, stopping to scrape paddle and bottom and sides of bowl. Add egg, beating well. Beat in vanilla.
5. In same medium bowl, whisk together flour, salt, cinnamon, and baking powder. Gradually add flour mixture to butter mixture, beating just until combined.
6. Spray a 9-inch round cake pan with baking spray with flour. Spoon large dollops (about 3 tablespoons) of brownie batter into bottom of prepared pan, leaving space between each. Crumble and sprinkle snickerdoodle dough between brownie dollops. Top with any remaining brownie batter and snickerdoodle dough. Tap pan on countertop to level batter and dough.
7. Bake until a wooden pick inserted in center comes out with a few crumbs, 30 to 35 minutes.
8. For topping: In a small bowl, whisk together sugar and cinnamon; sprinkle onto hot brookie. Let cool in pan for 15 to 20 minutes; best served warm. Store in an airtight container for up to 3 days.

Skillet S'mores Cookie

Makes 1 (10-inch) cookie

Bring a nostalgic camping treat indoors with this outrageously rich cookie that's studded with chunks of chocolate and toasted, melty marshmallows.

½ cup (113 grams) unsalted butter, softened
1⅓ cups (293 grams) firmly packed dark brown sugar
⅓ cup (67 grams) granulated sugar
1 large egg (50 grams), room temperature
1 large egg yolk (19 grams), room temperature
1 teaspoon (4 grams) vanilla extract
2⅔ cups (333 grams) all-purpose flour
1 teaspoon (5 grams) baking soda
1 teaspoon (3 grams) kosher salt
2 tablespoons (30 grams) heavy whipping cream, room temperature
1⅓ cups (220 grams) semisweet chocolate chips
2 sheets graham crackers (about 30 grams), broken into large pieces
1 (4.4-ounce) bar (125 grams) milk chocolate, broken into pieces and divided
6 to 8 marshmallows (44 to 58 grams)
⅓ cup (15 grams) miniature marshmallows

1. Position one oven rack in center and another oven rack in top third of oven. Preheat oven to 350°F (180°C). Spray a 10-inch cast-iron skillet with cooking spray.
2. In the bowl of a stand mixer fitted with the paddle attachment, beat butter and sugars at medium speed until fluffy, 3 to 4 minutes, stopping to scrape paddle and bottom and sides of bowl. Add egg, egg yolk, and vanilla, beating until combined.
3. In a medium bowl, whisk together flour, baking soda, and salt. With mixer on low speed, gradually add flour mixture to butter mixture, beating just until combined and stopping to scrape paddle and bottom and sides of bowl. Gradually beat in cream. Stir in chocolate chips.
4. Press half of dough (about 2 cups or 565 grams) into bottom of prepared skillet. Sprinkle graham cracker pieces onto dough. Dollop remaining dough in 2-teaspoon portions onto graham crackers. Using an offset spatula or the back of a spoon, gently spread dough only around sides of skillet. (Do not spread dough in center of skillet.) Tuck three-fourths of chocolate pieces between dollops of dough. Place skillet on center rack of oven; place a piece of foil on upper rack.
5. Bake until edges are set and center is dry, 40 to 45 minutes. Top with all marshmallows; broil in bottom rack of oven until marshmallows are puffed and toasted, about 2 minutes. Sprinkle remaining chocolate pieces onto hot cookie. Let cool on a wire rack for 30 minutes before serving. Store in an airtight container for up to 2 days.

Pro Tip

The foil on the upper oven rack helps prevents the sides of the cookie from overbaking before the center is done.

Butter Ring Cookies

Makes about 30 cookies

These cookies go by so many names—daisy flowers, flower cookies, butter rings—but the most nostalgic name to me is pinky ring cookies. When we were kids, my friends and I would slip our pinky finger through the hole in the cookie and play with it like a ring as we nibbled it off. If you know, you know!

½ cup (113 grams) unsalted butter, softened
½ cup (100 grams) granulated sugar
½ teaspoon (1.5 grams) kosher salt
1 large egg (50 grams), room temperature
½ teaspoon (2 grams) vanilla extract
2 cups (250 grams) all-purpose flour, plus more for dusting

1. In the bowl of a stand mixer fitted with the paddle attachment, beat butter, sugar, and salt at medium speed until smooth and creamy, 1 to 2 minutes, stopping to scrape paddle and bottom and sides of bowl. Beat in egg and vanilla until combined, stopping to scrape sides of bowl. With mixer on low speed, gradually add flour, beating just until combined and stopping to scrape paddle and bottom and sides of bowl.
2. Turn out dough onto a sheet of plastic wrap, and shape into a disk. Wrap in plastic wrap, and refrigerate until firm, about 1 hour.
3. Preheat oven to 350°F (180°C). Line baking sheets with parchment paper.
4. On a lightly floured surface, roll dough to 3⁄16-inch thickness. Using a 2¼-inch flower-shaped cutter, cut dough. Using a 1-inch round cutter, cut out center from flower shapes. Place cookies 1 inch apart on prepared pans. Reroll scraps, and cut to use all dough.
5. Bake until edges are lightly browned, 18 to 22 minutes. Let cool on pans for 10 minutes. Remove from pans, and let cool completely on wire racks. Store in an airtight container for up to 1 week.

Candy Compost Cookies and Bars

Makes about 12 bars or 24 cookies

When the dust settles after Halloween, Valentine's Day, or Easter, you've probably got more candy than you know what to do with. Consider this the grown-up solution to your kid candy surplus conundrum. This recipe can be made into cookies or bars with whatever candy you have on hand. No matter what you choose, you win.

- **½ cup (113 grams) unsalted butter, softened**
- **½ cup (110 grams) firmly packed light brown sugar**
- **3 tablespoons (36 grams) granulated sugar**
- **1 large egg (50 grams), room temperature**
- **½ teaspoon (2 grams) vanilla extract**
- **1⅔ cups (208 grams) all-purpose flour**
- **½ teaspoon (2.5 grams) baking powder**
- **½ teaspoon (2.5 grams) baking soda**
- **¼ teaspoon kosher salt**
- **2 tablespoons (30 grams) whole milk, room temperature**
- **1½ cups assorted chopped candy, divided**

1. In the bowl of a stand mixer fitted with the paddle attachment, beat butter and sugars at medium speed until fluffy, 3 to 4 minutes, stopping to scrape paddle and bottom and sides of bowl. Reduce mixer speed to medium-low. Add egg and vanilla, beating well.
2. In a medium bowl, whisk together flour, baking powder, baking soda, and salt. With mixer on low speed, gradually add flour mixture to butter mixture alternately with milk, beginning and ending with flour mixture, beating just until combined after each addition and stopping to scrape paddle and bottom and sides of bowl. Gently stir in ¾ cup candy. Refrigerate until slightly firm, about 30 minutes.
3. Preheat oven to 350°F (180°C).
4. For cookies: Line baking sheets with parchment paper. Using a 1½-tablespoon spring-loaded scoop, scoop dough, and place 2 inches apart on prepared pans. Top with remaining ¾ cup candy.
5. Bake until golden brown and fragrant, 10 to 12 minutes. Let cool on pans for 5 minutes. Remove from pans, and let cool completely on wire racks.
6. For bars: Line a 9-inch square baking pan with parchment paper, letting excess extend over sides of pan. Press dough into prepared pan. Top with remaining ¾ cup candy.
7. Bake until edges are golden brown and an instant-read thermometer inserted in center registers 200°F (93°C), about 30 minutes. Let cool in pan for 10 minutes. Using excess parchment as handles, remove from pan, and let cool completely on a wire rack before cutting into bars. Store cookies or bars in an airtight container for up to 3 days.

Peanut Butter-Marshmallow Skillet Cookie

Makes 1 (10-inch) cookie

Inspired by Fluffernutter—peanut butter and Marshmallow Fluff—sandwiches, this recipe perfectly balances sweet and salty flavors in one irresistible, melt-in-your-mouth cookie.

½ cup (113 grams) unsalted butter, softened
¾ cup (165 grams) firmly packed light brown sugar
1 large egg (50 grams)
2 large egg yolks (37 grams)
⅔ cup (170 grams) creamy peanut butter
1 tablespoon (21 grams) honey
1 teaspoon (4 grams) vanilla extract
1¾ cups (219 grams) all-purpose flour
½ cup (57 grams) coarsely chopped roasted unsalted peanuts
¾ teaspoon (3.75 grams) baking powder
¾ teaspoon (2.25 grams) kosher salt
½ teaspoon (2.5 grams) baking soda
Marshmallow Crème (recipe follows)
Garnish: flaked sea salt

1. Preheat oven to 325°F (170°C). Spray a 10-inch enamel-coated cast-iron skillet with baking spray with flour.
2. In the bowl of a stand mixer fitted with the paddle attachment, beat butter and brown sugar at medium speed until fluffy, 3 to 4 minutes, stopping to scrape paddle and bottom and sides of bowl. Add egg and egg yolks, one at a time, beating well after each addition. Add peanut butter, honey, and vanilla, beating until combined.
3. In a large bowl, stir together flour, peanuts, baking powder, kosher salt, and baking soda. With mixer on low speed, gradually add flour mixture to butter mixture, beating just until combined and stopping to scrape paddle and bottom and sides of bowl.
4. Spread 2½ cups (556 grams) dough into bottom and ¾ inch up sides of prepared skillet. Spread 3 cups (210 grams) Marshmallow Crème onto dough in skillet, leaving a ½-inch border around edges. Using a small spoon, dollop remaining dough all over Marshmallow Crème. Using a small offset spatula and short upward moves, drag dough into Marshmallow Crème to create a swirl as desired.
5. Bake until golden brown, about 40 minutes, loosely covering with foil during final 10 minutes of baking to prevent excess browning. Garnish with sea salt, if desired. Let cool on a wire rack for 20 minutes. Serve warm with remaining Marshmallow Crème. Store in an airtight container for up to 3 days.

Marshmallow Crème

Makes 5 cups

2 large egg whites (60 grams), room temperature
¾ cup (255 grams) light corn syrup
⅓ cup (67 grams) granulated sugar
½ teaspoon (1.5 grams) kosher salt
½ teaspoon (1 gram) cream of tartar
1½ teaspoons (6 grams) vanilla extract

1. In the top of a double boiler, whisk together egg whites, corn syrup, sugar, salt, and cream of tartar. Cook over simmering water, whisking constantly, until sugar dissolves and mixture registers 160°F (71°C) on an instant-read thermometer, about 7 minutes.
2. Carefully transfer mixture to the bowl of a stand mixer fitted with the whisk attachment, and beat at high speed until doubled in volume and stiff peaks form, 3 to 4 minutes. Beat in vanilla. Use immediately for preparing skillet cookie; store remainder for serving in an airtight container for up to 1 day.

LE CREUSET

index

credits

Editor-in-Chief Brian Hart Hoffman
EVP/Chief Content Officer Brooke Michael Bell
Editorial Director Nancy Meeks
Art Director Liz Kight
Senior Features Editor Amber Wilson
Assistant Editor Shelby Duffy
Baking and Pastry Editor Katie Moon Dickerson
Senior Copy Editor, Food Meg Lundberg
Senior Digital Imaging Specialist
Delisa McDaniel
Graphic Designer Kile Pointer

Test Kitchen Director Laura Crandall
Recipe Developers/Food Stylists
Ola Agbodza, Aaron Conrad,
Katie Moon Dickerson, Amanda Stabile

Photographers Jim Bathie, John O'Hagan,
Stephanie Welbourne Steele

Cover
Photography by Stephanie Welbourne Steele
Food Styling by Katie Moon Dickerson

about the author

A former flight attendant and self-taught baker, Brian Hart Hoffman spent his early life traveling and discovering bakeries around the world, returning home with a mission to re-create the recipes. Brian launched an award-winning brand dedicated to the celebration of the global baking community: *Bake from Scratch*. Now, *Bake from Scratch* is one of the world's largest baking platforms, with magazines and best-selling cookbooks, a podcast (*The Crumb*), sell-out international and domestic baking retreats, and, of course, @thebakefeed on Instagram, a way for bakers around the world to connect.

Brian has authored numerous best-selling books, including *The Coupe*, *Holiday Coupetails*, *Fast-Fix Baking*, *The Bread Collection*, *The Cake Collection*, *The Pie & Tart Collection*, *The Cookie Collection*, *The Bundt Collection*, *Another Bundt Collection*, *Holiday Cookies*, *It's Time to Bake Pastries*, and *Bake from Scratch: Artisan Recipes for the Home Baker* volumes 1–9.